Brother Deo Gratias

El glorioso S^t. Felix de Cantalicio
del Orden de Capuchinos lo mando ab-
rir un devoto especial del Santo en Cadiz
enel anno de 1772.

Brother Deo Gratias
St. Felix of Cantalice

BY

Lady Amabel Kerr

MEDIATRIX PRESS

MMXIX

ISBN: 978-1-953746-25-2

Layout provided by:
Ben Douglass

Cover art:

San Felice da Cantalice
Peter Paul Rubens
Cover design: Ben Douglass

Mediatrix Press
607 E. 6th Ave.
Post Falls, ID 83854

CONTENTS

CONTENTS

CHAPTER I

THE FARM LABOURER

ANTALICE, made memorable by giving its name to St. Felix, is perched up on the steep side of the valley of Rieti, in the Southern Apennines, its houses mingling with the rocks, where the line of cultivation ceases and that of forest waste begins. The Saint's biographers expatiate on the fairness of the broad valley beneath it, watered by the tortuous Vellino; though in their eyes its natural beauties pale before the significant fact that it had been hallowed three centuries before by the apostolate of St. Francis, who has left behind him what may be called indelible marks of his passage, at Rieti itself, at Greccio, at Fonte Colomba, and many other places in the vicinity of Cantalice.

Here then, under the Italian sky, in one of the most beautiful parts of our world, and on soil trodden by the blessed wounded feet of his seraphic father, St. Felix first saw the light. There is no certainty as to the date of his birth, for the only information on the subject rests on his own testimony. Even this is vague, for when, during his later years, he was asked his age, he replied that he did not know it for certain, but thought he must have been born in 1513, as he was almost sure he was about fourteen at the time of the Constable de Bourbon's sack of Rome in 1527.

In spite of the indifference which allowed his family and friends to forget the date of his birth, several distinct and graphic details about the circumstances of his early childhood have escaped oblivion. His father's name was Santi de' Porri, and only by this do we know that Felix possessed a surname, for never once, through the course of his long life, is it mentioned in

1

connection with him. Santi was a small farmer, possessed of a few acres of land, on the produce of which he and his family lived. His goats, which fed on the mountain side, supplied the simple household with milk, while from the wool of the sheep, Santa—for such was the name of Felix's mother—wove rough garments for her family. She and her husband were quiet, frugal, and domestic people, whose only care was to provide their little ones with the necessaries of life, and teach them such rudiments of religion as the *Pater*, *Ave*, and Ten Commandments. One member of the household, whose name is not mentioned, was better educated, and used to read aloud from the Gospels and Lives of the Saints when the work of the day was over. What he thus learnt made a deep impression on little Felix, and formed the theme of his meditations while he kept his father's sheep.

This Christian, patriarchal mode of life was in singular contrast with that of Santi's neighbours, who were remarkable, even in those disturbed days and in that southern clime, for the state of discord, brawling, and fighting, in which they lived. Their disorderly conduct drew down on them frequent punishments at the hands of the authorities of the Kingdom of Naples, and on account of the numerous fines to which the inhabitants were subjected, Cantalice was, when Felix was a child, in a very impoverished condition. Nor did the people become less quarrelsome as time went on, for many years later, when the Saint's name was a power before which even the treasury of the Church opened, he obtained an indulgence for his native village, to be gained by those only who pledged themselves to lead a peaceable life.

Little or nothing has been told us about the Saint's mother; but of his father we learn that he was a man of remarkable holiness, whose fidelity to grace was supernaturally rewarded by an interior premonition of the exact day of his death. His eldest son's child, an infant, named Santa after her grandmother, was dying; and as Santi knelt by the baby's side, speeding her on her way to heaven by his prayers, he said, so that all present heard him: "Go, Santarella, go now to the kingdom of heaven, and I will follow you on Saturday." At the time he spoke he was in apparently good health, but, true to his prediction, he sickened and died on the very day foretold by him.

The effect of the training of this family was lasting, and, in some cases at least, holiness was handed down to a third generation. Marco, son of Piermaria, Felix's youngest brother, led a most edifying life in Rome. One day, while devoutly going up the Scala Santa, he was seized with mortal illness. He at once made his way back to Cantalice, where, with a countenance radiant with joy, he announced to his relatives that he had come home to prepare for death, as his Uncle Felix, who had already entered into his glory, had appeared to him and called him to join him.

Felix was the third of four sons, Biagio and Carlo being his elders, and Piermaria as well as Potenza, the only daughter of the family, his juniors. Well named Felix, he was, even as a child, gifted with the happiest disposition, and gave no trouble during the few years he lived with his parents. Till he was nine years old he spent his time in keeping his father's sheep, and passed his days among the beautiful mountains, meditating in his childish way on the simple truths he had imbibed. Often, when permitted by his duties, he would kneel absorbed in prayer before a rough cross which he had cut on one of the oak trees which covered the slopes; and at times—as an earnest of the great austerities of his later life—the innocent child would hide in a thicket and discipline himself with a piece of rope.

His love of prayer could not remain concealed from the other little shepherds and shepherdesses of Cantalice, who, though they found his high moral standard very inconvenient, revered him for his piety. These children, if they were talking idly or sinfully, would cease when they saw him approaching. "Hush," they would say, "here comes Felix the Saint!" His presence, however, was not always a preventive of sin, and at times he saw and heard things which made him shudder. Then, if he could not escape from these bad little companions and retire to his beloved solitude, he would speak to them in grave but childish rebuke.

At the tender age of nine the little boy was put to live with and work for one Marco Pichi, who dwelt at Città Ducale, a town five miles south of Cantalice; and from henceforward he was a stranger to his own home. His parents may have thus sent him away on account of the evil companionship of the bad children with whom he was inevitably thrown; or they may have been driven to the step by necessity. They had more children at home than it was easy to support, and little Felix may have been compelled to work for his own living as soon as Piermaria was old enough to take his place with his father's flocks. This early separation from his mother's care entered visibly into the designs of Providence, for the hardships and detachment of his childhood trained him as nothing else could have done for his later life of holy toil.

Felix, however, found no hard master in Marco Pichi. Far from being harsh, the good man looked on himself as entirely responsible for the child's well-being, and, seeing at a glance that he was too small and young to undertake the labour in the fields for which he had been hired, he allowed him to do no hard work during his first years of service, but employed him to watch the sheep and cattle on the hills as he had been wont to do for his father. When, at the end of twenty years, Felix left Marco's employ, their parting was more like that between father and son than between master and servant.

Shepherds from the times of Abel and David the King have ever been the favourites of God; and in all ages of Christianity, from Christmas night down to more modern times, we find Him choosing them as the recipients of His secrets. Felix was no exception in this divine predilection, and the things of God which he learnt among the solitudes of the hills, and expressed in rough canticles, remained with him till latest old age. He was, however, taken from his life of contemplation ere childhood had merged itself in boyhood; and being brought by his master to live under his roof with his other servants and work with them in the fields, Felix thenceforward had to seek God in the daily drudgery of labour and in the company of coarse-minded, unsympathetic men. Yet he found Him whom he sought.

We know Felix as a great saint, moving men's hearts to God, and endowed by Him with a rare gift of working miracles; but he won his way to sanctity and prepared his soul for supernatural gifts by the faithful performance of the arduous, monotonous, unelevating duties of a farm labourer. For twenty years did he look after his master's business with scrupulous exactitude, never neglecting a duty, never wasting a moment; and when at length God called him to a higher life, the Saint had already been moulded to His hand by years of fidelity to duty.

Needless to say that he who lived for God alone, began and ended his daily toil with Him; and however early he might rise, or however late he retired to rest, Felix never failed to say his prayers on his knees. The boy shared one dormitory in common with all the men-servants of Marco's establishment, and when he was first put to sleep there the rebuke conveyed to them by his devout ways was very displeasing to his fellows. "So you want to make yourself out a saint, do you?" said they tauntingly. "Don't you pretend to be any better than us. We will not believe it even if you work miracles!" Still more angry were they when he knelt down to say his grace before and after meals, a pious habit which he had probably brought with him from his Christian home.

But Felix's soul had been taught of God in solitude, and, however cheerfully he accommodated himself to the companionship of his rude fellow-servants, his desire to be alone became so imperative that he found the means of satisfying it. There was under the roof a small cupboard-like room which he was allowed to appropriate to his own use, and fit up with his only earthly possessions, namely, a little lead crucifix, and three common prints of our Lady, St. Francis, and St Bonaventure. The memory of this cell was always dear to him, and even in later years he spoke with affection of "that little garret in his master's house which he would not have exchanged for the grandest hall in the Vatican." Thither he stole after his fellow-servants were asleep, and there he spent the night in prayer, and in mortifications which already began to be heroic.

Soon the difference in his mode of life from theirs was made still more apparent to his fellow-servants, than when his only singularity was saying his prayers on his knees. The way he passed his nights in his cell was an open secret; and his daily life was marked by an abstemiousness which was incomprehensible to them. Not only did he refuse to consider himself dispensed by age or condition from observing the ordinary fasts of the Church, but he touched nothing but bread and water on the vigils of feasts, and was always so sparing in his diet that it seemed to his fellows that he kept a perpetual fast. In spite, however, of these practices—which the members of Marco's household unanimously condemned—there was something so winning about the boy as they grew to know him better, that they found it impossible to quarrel with him. However harshly they might speak to him, they could never extort an angry reply; and, instead of resenting the extra work they put on him, he was always ready to offer his help, and undertake more than his right share.

He kept a most severe guard over his tongue, and, far from joining in the idle, if not mischievous, talk of his companions, he rarely spoke unless first spoken to, though his manner was so pleasant that no one felt rebuffed by his reticence. When asked the reason of this habitual reserve, he replied simply that he thought his tongue had been given to him for only good and useful purposes. Not but what there were times when he used it freely, for he did not spare his fellow-servants if they spoke profanely. The first time he heard one of his companions blaspheme he cried out—child as he was—with holy horror: "What are you doing? You are offending God! Are you not afraid that the earth will swallow you up? Quick! quick! run to the church and ask God to forgive you." At first his fellows resented such reproaches, but by degrees, as his gentle, unselfish ways won their affection, they accepted his rebukes, and vouchsafed a kindly tolerance of all his pious eccentricities.

Sundays and feasts—carefully observed in Marco's house— were days of joy as well as rest to Felix. He always approached the sacraments on Sunday, and the careful devotion of his manner when receiving Communion was observed and recorded. His greatest desire was to hear Mass daily. This was made impossible by the routine of his laborious life, but not a day passed without his hearing Mass spiritually—nay, more, he at times heard it in the body also. There were people ready to swear that they had seen him on his knees in the church, while others could have equally sworn that they had at the same moment seen him working in the fields. This presence of Felix in two places at once, and the conviction that he who was working while the holy youth was praying could be none other than his guardian angel, deepened the feeling towards him from kindliness to reverence.

On Sundays, after hearing Mass, he retired to his beloved little cell. But as he grew from boyhood to manhood he felt a want in his communion with God which he had not known before. He loved prayer, and his soul spoke very straight to God, but the time came when he craved for food for prayer such as he might have found in spiritual books. All books were sealed to him, for he never to the end of his life learned to read. In later years men were so astounded to hear him repeating long passages from Scripture and the liturgy, of which by that time his retentive memory was a veritable storehouse, that they were inclined to disbelieve his professions of ignorance. "How should I have ever learned to read?" he replied to one such doubter. "How do you think a poor peasant who spent his boyhood keeping sheep, and grew up with nothing but spades and pitchforks in his hand, could have learnt his letters? Nor, since I have been in Rome, have I had time or thought for anything save my wallet and gourd. No, no, I can read no book but my crucifix."

When he spoke those words, his extraordinary oral knowledge of the Divine Office had supplied his spiritual needs, but while in Marco's service he had found no substitute for books, and probably missed the evening readings of his early life at home. He was not, however, suffered to feel the want for long, before a remedy was supplied. One of his fellow-servants, Giambattista, was a relative of his, and on him the example and simple holiness of Felix produced such an effect as to change his whole life and develop a vocation for the priesthood. He now came to his kinsman's relief, and used to go with him to his little cell after Mass on Sundays and there read aloud.

Their book, by predilection, *was The Lives of the Fathers of the Desert*, which, while no doubt it fostered the piety of

Giambattista, had a still more powerful effect on Felix. For twenty years had he been leading his holy life of service and sanctifying his state of labour, and the time had now come when he, who had been so faithful in that which was less, was ripe to receive those things which are greater. During his days of labour and nights of prayer he had been gradually penetrating the secrets of God, and by his twenty years of faithful work and service he had laid the fuel to which it now remained for the Holy Ghost to apply the kindling spark. As Felix listened with absorbed attention to the record of the lives of those grand saints of the early centuries, and drank in the spiritual counsels with which their chronicles abound, nothing—he thought—would satisfy him but to try to imitate them literally as a solitary in some unfrequented nook in his native mountains.

But almost simultaneously with this desire there arose in his mind a consideration which quenched it. It was not pusillanimity—far from it. Solitude had charms for this simple labouring man which nothing else possessed, and as for austerities, his fasts, vigils and self-macerations had for years emulated those of the holy fathers, in whose footsteps he wished to tread. The one thing in the life of a hermit of which he was afraid was its liberty, and its absence of all responsibility towards a superior. He who had been for so many years climbing towards sanctity by means of ordinary obedience to an earthly master, felt convinced that, if God bade him go higher, it must be higher in the same direction in which he had already walked, and that, to be perfect, he must exchange ordinary for religious obedience.

CHAPTER II

THE CALL TO GO HIGHER

ABOUT fifteen years after the birth of Felix, Matthew Braschi had been moved by the Holy Ghost to found the reformed branch of the great Order of St. Francis, known ever since by the name of Capuchin. This name, given to the friars on account of the hoods they wore, in accordance with what they held to be the primitive Franciscan rule, was illustrative of their desire to carry out the intentions of their seraphic father in small things as well as in great, and to be as like him in the habits they wore as in their spirit of holy poverty. No sooner had the reformed Order received the sanction of Clement VII than it spread itself over Italy, taking root in every part, and working wonders for the salvation and sanctification of souls. The friars had planted themselves among other places at Città Ducale, where St. Felix must often have seen them; and as soon as the interior voice had told him that it was not his vocation to be a hermit among the fastnesses of the Apennines, he turned his thoughts to these sons of St. Francis.

Without hesitation Felix told his cousin that he had made up his mind, not only to leave the world, but to offer himself as a lay-brother to the Capuchins. Giambattista was not of the same opinion as his simple-minded kinsman, and did his best to persuade him that his vocation was to go on serving God in the world as he had hitherto done; but Felix was not to be moved from his decision. Equally firm was he when his cousin tried to induce him to choose some less severe Order; for the austerities and poverty of the early Capuchins frightened those who were acquainted with their ways. He might as well have spoken to a

9

stone. "If I enter religion at all, I will choose the most perfect way," Felix maintained. "It is better to leave a thing alone than not do it thoroughly. With me it must be all or nothing!" With this axiom, which was henceforward to govern his life, Felix closed the argument, for Giambattista held his peace, having no wish to fight against God.

Though convinced as to his true vocation, Felix hesitated to follow it, his hesitation being due, it would seem, to purely earthly motives. He loved his master and was grateful for the kindness he had received at his hands, and knew, moreover, how valuable his services had become to him. Thus, from dread of paining Marco, or of seeming thankless towards him, he delayed telling him of his decision and obtaining his discharge. This want of prompt obedience to the divine call was—as Felix was afterwards convinced—displeasing to God, and he regarded an accident which befell him soon after as a punishment inflicted to compel his obedience.

He was asked by a neighbour to break in two young oxen to the plough. Ever ready to be of service, he willingly assented, and, crossing the Vellino, set to work to harness them. Marco, meanwhile, stood in his own field, on the other side of the river, and watched the proceedings with interest. No sooner had Felix succeeded in fastening the young beasts to the yoke and had taken hold of the handle to guide the plough than they became unmanageable. He ran to their heads, but they bore him to the ground and galloped over him, dragging the plough after them. All present felt sure that Felix must be killed, or, at least, terribly mangled by the plough-share; and they were amazed to see him rise to his feet uninjured, though with his clothes torn into ribbons. Then they saw him fall on his knees in prayer. As he had lain under the hoofs of the oxen, in imminent danger of death, Felix had understood the accident to be a manifestation of God's displeasure; and the moment the peril was over, he knelt down and surrendered himself to the divine will. "I understand, Lord," he said, "I understand what Thou wantest of me. I will obey Thee this very moment. Have patience with me while I settle my affairs."

Marco had hastened across the river, and, folding his ploughman in his arms, thanked God aloud for what he could not but regard as his miraculous preservation. "Go home, my son," said he, "go home and change your clothes and I will follow." But Felix would not leave the spot till he had told his master that he must quit his service for a higher life. Marco went round telling all his neighbours about the accident, and they hastened in numbers to his house to convince themselves with their own eyes that the labourer they all knew so well was alive. They all, however, mourned when they learned that they were to lose him from Città Ducale.

The day of his departure from Marco's house arrived, and Felix received the wages which were due to him. With scrupulous honesty he asked his master to keep back the price of two glasses of wine and a wisp of hay which he had—we may presume lawfully—given away out of the stores under his charge, and begged him to distribute the residue among the poor in the town. His father and mother had ere this gone to reap the reward of their labours in a better world, but his other relatives remained, and his fellow-servants reproached Felix for not giving his money to them. "It is by the counsel of God that I act thus," he replied. "I must obey Him."

Before he left his master's service he paid one visit to Cantalice to announce his intention to his kinsfolk and bid them farewell. His brothers, like Giambattista, were alarmed by the severity of the Order chosen by Felix, and begged him to reconsider his decision and be content with some less rigorous way of serving God. "I will do this or nothing," he replied. "Do you pray to God to help me, for I tell you that you will never see me again except in a Capuchin habit." And with these words he turned his back on Cantalice, to visit it only once more before his death.

There was something very patriarchal in the manner of this faithful servant's parting from the family he had served so devotedly. When he took his leave he knelt before Marco and his wife, and asked their pardon for all his offences against them during the past twenty years and promised to pray for them as long as he lived. "I thank you, master," said he, "for the way you have treated me, and for the fatherly love you have had for me from the time I entered your service as a child, even to this hour. Now, Master Marco, give me your blessing as though I were in truth your son."

Marco's wife and children here began to weep, and Marco himself replied: "My Felix, I have indeed loved and cherished you as a son. I have never found a fault in you, and have always been satisfied with your faithful service. Indeed, I could not consent to your leaving me, were you not going to give yourself to God in the religious life." Then, having given him his blessing, he folded him in his arms, saying: "Farewell, my Felix, farewell;" and could speak no more on account of his emotion. Then, one by one, the family embraced the faithful servant, and were so loth to let him go that they accompanied him through the streets and would not leave him till the convent gate closed on him.

The only reason which took Felix to the Capuchins' house at Città Ducale was to ascertain how he was to gain admission as lay-brother in some more distant convent of the Order; for he had no desire to remain near his former home. Dwelling as he did in the same little town with him, the Father Guardian had most probably heard Felix spoken of, but was not personally acquainted with him, and showed no alacrity to receive him. Whether his suspicions were roused by the farm-servant's reputation for holiness, or whether he only wished to prove the reality of a sanctity which he could not fail to perceive, he at once put Felix's sincerity and humility to a severe test. Without showing him the slightest sympathy, he roughly reproached the applicant for leaving his master's service, and attributed his desire for the religious life to love of novelty and the wish to be quit of a life of labour. "We do not want that sort of man," he concluded by saying, "and the sooner you go back to the plough the better."

Felix accepted the reproaches not only humbly but simply. "God forbid, father," he replied with an honesty which carried conviction with it, "that any such motives should bring me here. God alone has moved me to ask admission as a lay-brother, and

I call Him to witness that I have no object in view except my salvation."

The Father Guardian was pleased with this answer, but resolved to put Felix to a further test. Taking him into the church, he placed him before a crucifix, and, having drawn a vivid picture of the hardships and austerities of a Capuchin's life, asked if he were willing to suffer this, and more besides, for the sake of Jesus Christ crucified. Felix had remained unmoved when he parted from his master's family, and had shed no tears in response to theirs, but now, as he looked at the image of his crucified Lord, the tenderness of his heart overcame him, and he fell on his knees weeping.

"Ah, no, father," he cried, "I fear neither difficulties nor sufferings, whether they come from the rule or from any other cause. I can do all things through Him who strengthens me." The Guardian was now satisfied in his own mind as to the reality of the holy labourer's vocation, and sent him to Rome with a letter of introduction.

But the difficulties in the way of Felix's vocation were not yet over. When the Vicar-Provincial, Raphael of Volterra, saw him, he was not prepossessed in his favour, and pronounced him to be too old for acceptance as a lay-brother. He was but thirty, but, no doubt, his exposure to all weathers since early childhood, and his constant toil with plough, hoe, and spade, had aged him beyond his years, bowed his back and banished any remaining appearance of youth from his countenance. When, however, he began to speak, Volterra was struck by his manner, and feared lest he might be guilty of rashness if he rejected him. He consulted the Father Guardian, Bernardine of Asti, and together they arrived at the conclusion—so blessed to their Order and to Rome—to accept him in spite of any disadvantages of which he might be possessed.

Once accepted, Felix was sent to make his novitiate at Anticole; but before sending him away Father Volterra advised him to sell all he had and give to the poor. This had already been done, and when he had stood begging for admission to the house of St. Francis, no one on earth could have been poorer than he.

The desire of Felix's soul was now granted; and the crown was put to his joy when, eight days after his arrival at the novitiate, he received the habit of St. Francis. Contrary to custom, he kept in religion his baptismal name, which was so suited to his joyous disposition in time, and prophetic of his blessed state in eternity. But in spite of his identity in name, he knew and felt that henceforward he must be a new man, and thus apostrophized himself: "You are no longer that Felix born of flesh and blood, who ate, drank, and lived among men. You must put on an altogether new Felix. You must cease to live for yourself and must live only for God. The habit which you have received must teach you every moment you wear it that you have become the disciple of Jesus crucified, which means that you must die to the world and crucify the flesh." Thus saying, he commanded not only his senses but even his thoughts to obey this new Felix, and occupy themselves solely about the things of God; and rarely have senses and thoughts been found as obedient to the will as Felix's proved to be.

But his novitiate, on which he entered so joyously, was destined to bring with it trials which probably he had not anticipated. His life of retreat and introspection exposed him to temptations to which he had hitherto been too busy to give ear. The devil scourged the simple servant of God with the foulest suggestions and imaginations, and even taught him evil things about which he had hitherto remained ignorant. Humility and prayer were Felix's weapons, and before these the enemy of mankind never holds his ground for long. Ere his twelvemonth's novitiate was over, the servant of God had recovered his peace of soul, never more to lose it.

The struggle, however, had worn him out, and his body, inured to every kind of physical toil, succumbed under the unwonted strain of mental anguish, and fell a prey to low fever. Little accustomed to study his health, Felix looked on the languor and depression consequent on the fever as a new form of temptation, and fought it as energetically as he had fought those of a grosser kind. But one thing troubled him. The Capuchin rule was most stringent in its prohibition against admitting to profession any novice whose health gave cause for anxiety; and, seeing the severity of a Capuchin's life, this precaution was absolutely necessary. Felix obviously feared lest, at the end of his novitiate, he might be rejected on the score of weak health, and sent up fervent prayers to God and to his holy father, St. Francis, to whom his devotion grew as he imitated his life more closely.

When the time came his fears were likely to be realised, for half the Community declared that it would be madness to accept one so shattered in health. The other half, however, urged his profession, and, fortunately, had their way. There were those among the friars who, by close observation of the humble novice, were assured that they had a saint dwelling in their midst; and the arguments of these prevailed over those of the more cautious.

For the next three years Felix dwelt in the convent at Tivoli, where strength of mind and body were fully restored to him. Little or nothing has been recorded of those three years in the Saint's life, during which he had leisure to devote himself entirely to the care of his soul, and advance in the spiritual life; but it is certain that it was during that time that he drank in the heavenly wisdom and learnt the divine secrets which he spent the remaining forty years of his life in imparting to those with whom he came in contact. All in the convent at Tivoli wondered how a man taken straight from the plough and unable even to read or write had come to be such a master of the spiritual life.

CERCA IL DISPREZZO IL NERI IN SANTA GARA
COL BUON FELICE IN MEZZO A POPOL FOLTO,
E L' UN DA L' ALTRO E UMILTADE IMPARA,
BELLO IL SEMBRAR PER UMILTADE STOLTO.

(1) S. Filippo dalla strada de' banchi beve alla Lacca di S. Felice Cappuccino
mendico, coperto col suo proprio capello.

N.º 34

CHAPTER III

THE FOUR INITIAL VIRTUES

N THE year 1547, when Felix had been three years at Tivoli, he was summoned to Rome to act as assistant collector of alms. It happened, however, that Brother Angelo, the old friar with whom it had been intended he should work, died shortly after, and left his colleague in sole charge of the organisation for providing necessaries for the Community and those dependent on it, which forms such a large part of a Capuchin lay-brother's vocation. Once undertaken, it was God's design for Felix that he should persevere in this one charge for forty years, at the end of which death alone relieved him of it.

It is a difficult task to follow the Saint through the holy monotony of the remainder of his life, unrelieved by lights and shadows, and devoid of those epochs by which we are wont to measure time. Day by day he followed a fixed routine from which he rarely departed except on feasts, which had, for him, a special monotony of their own. He took up his work, duly meted out, in the morning, and repeated it week after week, year after year, beginning it again and again with renewed fervour, and growing visibly in holiness though all else was unchanged.

To himself the difference of this life from that which he had been leading at Tivoli was great, for his solitude and uninterrupted communion with God were exchanged for a life of ceaseless intercourse with men. He was not even allowed to try to realise the ideal, in its more literal sense, of living in the world without being of the world; for his new duties involved active conversation with those of whom he begged. If he had failed in this he would have done his work badly.

When, on being first summoned to Rome, he faced in all its aspects the mode of life which was to be his for the future, he at once grasped its supernatural side, and understood that the life of a collecting-brother must be regarded as a distinct religious vocation. He therefore lost no time in trying to sanctify the life and cultivate the virtues essentially belonging to his state. These he put under four heads: recollection in the midst of publicity, obedience, diligence and poverty. At the time he saw nothing beyond these four, for his humility blinded him to the possible developments of his vocation. Little did he foresee that the faithful and holy performance of his daily task of tramping through the streets of Rome, knocking at the doors of benefactors, and filling his wallets and gourds with provisions bestowed by charity, would shape itself into an apostolate only second to, and uniting itself with, that of St. Philip, the Apostle of Rome.

He saw nothing of this yet, and his only present care was how to save and sanctify his own soul in his new, distracting vocation, and carry out its duties exactly according to God's will. He took his solitude with him into the crowded streets and squares, and walked about in a state of silence and recollection. Nevertheless, when called on to speak he always had a pleasant remark ready, usually seasoned with a spice of shrewd advice, which won the hearer's heart while it conveyed its lesson. He habitually held his rosary in his hand as he walked about, and often said it aloud, though so deeply did he enter into the meaning of the holy words that time after time he got no further than one Hail Mary. Sometimes, carried away by devotion, he would stand still before one of the many pictures of our Lady at the corners of the streets, and pray aloud to her. "Dear Mother," he was overheard on one occasion to say, "I commend poor Brother Felix to your care. He desires to love you and be a good son to you. Do not refuse to stretch out your hand to help him, for he is like a little child who cannot walk alone."

St. Felix was habitually accompanied by another brother, but this in no way interfered with his silence and solitude. He assured Brother Alessio, his usual companion during the earlier years of his life in Rome, that, as they went about begging solely by obedience, their occupation need not in any way interfere with their prayers or recollection. Lay-brothers, he went on to explain, had to preach by their actions, while the priests of the Order preached from the pulpit.

"Come, brother," said he one day to Brother Marco, during a time of public revelry; "let us go and preach in the city." With eyes cast down and hands folded the two brothers walked slowly through the public streets without saying a word, save when they responded to the salutation of their acquaintances by the simple ejaculation: *Deo Gratias.* "Have you forgotten the sermon, brother?" asked Marco, when they reached the convent door on their return. "No," replied the Saint, "I have not forgotten. We have been preaching all the time we were walking along." This incident of St. Felix's "walking sermon" is illustrative of one of the many ways in which he loved to imitate, in the most literal manner, the actions of his holy father St. Francis.

His obedience was most perfect. When he took up the work of collecting he found that the brothers employed in it had to a certain extent emancipated themselves from the obedience enjoined by the rule. They went where they chose, asked for what seemed best to them, and, furthermore, distributed what they had collected entirely according to their own discretion. Apparently no one perceived this, or found fault with the course adopted by the truly holy friars who preceded Felix in the office. The actual state of things did not, however, receive like toleration from the Saint himself, and the same religious spirit which made him relinquish the idea of a hermit-life, now made him rule his daily duties by strict obedience. Never did he start on his rounds without obtaining due permissions and limitations from his superiors. On one occasion his request for direction was met by a general permission to do as he wished. "No, no," he cried, "it is not for me to have a choice. You must command; I must obey. Do not forget that I am but as the ass of the Community; and what confusion would there not arise were the ass to dictate to its master how it was to be laden, and how employed!"

When a command of any kind was given him he was so blind in his obedience as to be willing to attempt impossibilities at its

bidding. Hence it passed into a byword among the friars that
each one must measure his words, and take heed to what he said
in the hearing of Brother Felix, lest he should see a command
where none was intended. The greatest proof of his love of holy
obedience was that he brought under its control even his insatia-
ble thirst for suffering, so that not one of his heroic austerities
was undertaken except by permission.

One of the many forms of mortification adopted by St. Felix
was that of going about bare-foot. This was in accordance with
the primitive custom of the Capuchins, though in the Saint's time
the friars wore sandals, by virtue of a dispensation which had
followed closely on the rule itself. He continued with the more
severe practice till late old age, though before his last illness he
proved how willing he was to abandon even this at the call of
obedience. Not long before his death he and Brother Matteo—his
colleague during the last twenty years of his life—were waiting
on Cardinal Santorio, the protector of the Order. Matteo, without
much consideration, complained to the Cardinal that Felix, at his
advanced age, should be allowed to go barefoot in all seasons;
whereupon Santorio, equally without deliberation, commanded
the old friar to wear sandals henceforward. This obedience cost
St. Felix much; yet he never hesitated in complying with it. As
soon as he returned home he told the Father Guardian what he
had been commanded to do. The sandals, however, had to be
made for him, and there was some undue delay in their comple-
tion; and the Saint's mind was really tormented by his apparent
disobedience. To pacify him his superiors had to impose on him
the counter obedience of accepting the situation with peace
of mind.

It is not easy to describe the manner in which he practised
the virtue of diligence—the third which he imposed on himself—
for it was the normal condition of his religious life, even as
industry of a more natural order had been that of his life in the
world. Not only did he do his own work untiringly, but, when he
could, he took on him that of others. When there was a choice,
he always claimed the heaviest load and the hardest task for
himself, and—disclaiming what he considered the too respectful

name of Brother—he styled and regarded himself as the ass of the Community. Truly, were any one in these days to treat his ass as Felix treated himself, he would speedily find himself subjected to punishment for cruelty to animals. "Make way for the donkey," he would say, when he came across an obstruction on the road; and when—before they became accustomed to the pleasantry—people asked him where the beast was, he, pointing to himself, would reply: "What! don't you know the Capuchins' ass?"

This likening of himself to an ass which has to be made to work, without merit on its part, but simply—as he put it—because it has been created by God to labour in the same way that a vine is created to bear grapes, became almost the initial idea of St. Felix's life. We find him recurring to it on every occasion. Thus, one day, being heavily laden with well-filled wallets and gourds, he fell down in the mud, and could not rise on account of his encumbrances. He called to his companion, who had walked on unconscious of the accident: "Come back," he cried. "What are you about? Do you not see that the donkey has fallen? Come and give him a good thrashing to make him get up!"

When, as rarely happened, the Saint fell ill, and was really unable to work, he was most unwilling to yield to his weakness; and, true to his prevailing idea, assured the infirmarian that the donkey was only jibbing, and required nothing but a good beating to make him go on again. "For," he would add, "asses must be made to go whether they wish it or no."

"Old father," said one of the younger brothers to him as he watched him pursuing his usual duties, though evidently spent with fatigue, "you look pale and languid. Are you ill?" "Ill?" returned the Saint. "Not I! I am well enough; but greedy old asses must be punished sometimes by feeling the weight of their work." In fact, so completely did St. Felix identify himself with a beast of burden, that even when he was dying he could not resist making the usual comparison. "Ah," said he, when the infirmarian lifted him from the ground and laid him on the bed which he was never again to leave, "this time the Capuchins' ass has fallen so heavily that it will never more get on its legs."

So devoted was the Saint to the accomplishment of his arduous work that he told a friend that he felt ashamed when any other duty made him appear in the streets without his wallet on his shoulder. "They are my ornaments, my wreaths of flowers," he said gaily, in allusion to his heavy burdens, speaking thus in response to the commiserations of one who had found him, waiting outside a door, bowed down under their weight.

After the Cardinal-protector had been persuaded to command St. Felix to wear sandals, it occurred to him that it was high time for the holy old man to be relieved altogether from his work as collector. "What think you," he said to the Saint one day, when the latter was calling for alms at the Cardinal's palace; "what think you of an idea I have of ministering to your weakness and relieving you of your work, so that you may have more leisure to attend to your soul before you die?" Now, the Cardinal had on more than one occasion shown a tendency to exceed his powers as protector, and each time this had happened St. Felix had shown himself most tenacious of the rights of his Order. His present reply was actuated by his dislike to undue interference, as well as by his reluctance to accept alleviations.

"What weakness do you mean?" he exclaimed. "God forbid that I should be relieved by you of any of my work! I pray you, Monsignor, to let me be ruled and guided by my superiors, at whose disposal I left myself when I took my vows. They must know what I am capable of doing far better than you can. Were they to allow me to die under my burden I should not feel aggrieved, for thus does it befit an ass to die. Know, Monsignor, that my daily task, which you say exhausts my strength, is dearer to me than your most costly possessions could be to you. The wallet on my shoulder, laden with alms, makes me think I am carrying my Saviour's Cross; and had I the good fortune to die under its weight I should rejoice."

It was remarked of St. Felix that he could not be idle for even a minute. If the weather, or any other impediment, kept him from making his rounds, he spent his time working in the garden; or, if compelled to remain indoors, he occupied himself by making little wooden crosses, which he distributed among the benefactors of the Community, to promote devotion to our Lord crucified. He did not realise that he was at the same time promoting devotion to himself; for as his reputation of sanctity increased, rich and poor alike were anxious to possess these crosses for the sake of him who made them.

His idea of what religious poverty should be is thus pithily summed up by himself: "It is true that I was born and bred a poor, a very poor, peasant; but I was not half as poor as a Friar Minor ought to be." Poverty, as the chosen bride of his holy father St. Francis, was of all virtues most dear to him; and he declared that a much-patched habit was the most glorious livery that a Franciscan could wear. Poverty assumed a personality to him such as she had assumed to his seraphic father, and seemed to preside over his actions. During a time of great scarcity the Father Guardian of the Capuchin convent was so afraid lest the friars should find themselves in want that he bade St. Felix to do his best to collect alms even more than sufficient for their present need. "I will obey," replied the Saint, "but believe me, father, our beloved mother poverty weeps when her children have abundance."

His love of holy poverty, and his resolve to be in every way faithful to the chosen spouse of St. Francis, made him seek out the worst of everything for his own use. In the earlier days of the Capuchin reform the friars wore habits made of a sort of sackcloth, such as was used for galley-slaves. This, however, had been abandoned for serge, on account of the more durable qualities of the latter. There was among the convent stores a cast-off habit of the former pattern, and this St. Felix begged to have for his own use, though his companions assured him that it would be an economy to wear a serge habit. He replied that whether his tunic lasted a long or short time was nothing to the purpose; he preferred the sackcloth because it was a commoner and poorer article.

No one, however, could have complained that St. Felix's habit did not last him a sufficiently long time, for he wore it till it literally dropped off him; and, from the frequent cutting off torn fragments and sewing up rents, it was in the end ludicrously short and narrow. As for his cloak, it was so patched that it would have defied any one to find out which was the original material.

He carried the same poverty into his cell, where he combined his love of this virtue with his love of austerity. A bare board with an old coverlid, and a faggot of vine tendrils for a pillow, composed his bed; for it was only in late old age that obedience compelled him to lie on a palliasse, if that name could be given to a bag of straw such as a man could carry under one arm. In a corner a table stood, on which lay some bundles of wood, the material for his little crosses, and a large knife with which he carved them; while near these was the big stick he carried about with him to knock at the doors of those of whom he solicited alms. There was no other furniture in the cell, but overhead there hung from the ceiling his wallets and wine gourds, and some odds and ends of old pieces of stuff used by him indiscriminately to patch his habit and wipe himself with when he came in from his long and laborious rounds. The rule provided that linen cloths should be allowed to the begging-brothers for this purpose, but the Saint waived the permission and used these old woolen rags, adding that they were too good, as a wisp of straw ought to suffice to rub down an ass.

This cell, the walls of which are made of wattled reeds and twigs daubed with clay and lime, enclosing a space of about eight feet square, can still be seen. The Capuchin convent where St. Felix dwelt was attached to the Church of Santa Croce, in the Via dei Lucchesi; but when the Community moved to the new church in the Piazza Barberini, not only were the Saint's relics removed there, but with them the slender structure wherein he had dwelt.

Whether from acquaintance with St. Francis's urgent injunctions on the subject, or from a mere filial instinct, St. Felix detested the very sight of money, and would not be persuaded to touch it. Though it was the business of his life to collect the worth of money from benefactors, it was known to them that he would not take a coin as an alms. This habit was, on one occasion, turned into the subject of a practical joke. He was waylaid in front of the Church of Sant' Eustachio by some students of the German College, for whom he had a great affection. While talking with them and—as was his wont—making them sing hymns with him, one of the youths dropped a small piece of money into the Saint's wallet. At once it became preternaturally heavy. "What is this?" he exclaimed. "Good Lord, have mercy on me! A serpent must be in my bag!" Hurrying into the entrance of the church he turned out the contents of his wallet, and the coin rolled into the gutter—where he left it.

CHAPTER IV

PENANCE AND JOY

ACH of these four initial virtues, in the faithful cultivation of which St. Felix hoped to find a safeguard against the distractions of intercourse with the world, brought in its train special mortifications; though what has been related in the last chapter can give no idea of his life of heroic penance. That his austerities should be heroic was to be expected of one to whom, even as innocent shepherd-boy and toil-worn farm-servant, penance was the one road whereon he believed perfection to lie. It is related by the Saint's biographers that all his austerities were ruled by obedience, and it is well to remember this when we read in what they consisted, both because of the additional splendour which it sheds on his own sanctity, and because of the light it throws on the spirit of the Capuchin reform.

St. Felix's fasts rivalled those of his beloved Fathers of the desert. Besides the Lent of the Church, he observed most rigorously what are called St. Francis's four Lents, by which the season of fasting is practically extended over three-fourths of the year. In addition to this he fasted on bread and water all the year round on three days out of every week; and it was observed that no food or drink of any sort passed his lips during the last three days of Holy Week. Herbs were his nourishment by predilection, though obedience compelled him to take other things.

Very often his duties in the city kept him out till after the hour for supper in the refectory; and then, if he could do so without being observed, he would go to his cell without the meal. If, however, he found himself compelled to eat what had been set

27

aside for him, he mixed with it ashes from the kitchen fire. It is scarcely necessary to say that never, either in winter chills or summer heats, would he accept the hospitality pressed on him by those from whom he received alms. But he was human; and the one occasion when the flesh overcame him and caused him to commit what he bewailed as a heinous offence against God, does much to show us the merit of his habitual abstinence.

One evening he returned home very late, and, feeling exhausted from want of food, he told his companion, Brother Alessio, to cut some bacon from a piece which formed part of the alms they had collected, and give him some, while he ate some himself. Barely, however, had St. Felix tasted it before he was filled with remorse for what he called his gluttony. "Alas, brother," he cried, "that we should have been so cowardly as to yield to such slight temptation. Let us hasten to do penance!" This took place on a Wednesday evening, and till the end of the week he tasted no food at all, in reparation for his momentary fall.

The severity of his sanguinary disciplines made those shudder who watched him unobserved, in the manner which will be related in another chapter. There were other mortifications which he could not attempt to conceal—such, for instance, as his visit to the seven churches which he made bare-foot every Sunday—his one day of rest. Unknown to men, he added to the penance of fatigue by wearing under his habit a terrible breast-plate armed with iron spikes which lacerated his flesh as he walked along. He contrived to keep this means of penance secret till after his death, for he left the instrument of torture in the care of a Franciscan Tertiary, Sister Felice, at whose house he called to put it on, either before he made his Sunday pilgrimage, or whenever public calamities or disorders moved him to the practice of more severe penance. Sister Felice kept his secret loyally, and had the breast-plate in her charge at the time of the Saint's death, when she was persuaded to give it to Lorenzo Ferrara, who venerated it as a most precious relic.

With St. Felix, as with many other saints whose vocation made them mix with the world, it was by turning to an ingenious account the daily events of his life, rather than by such extraordinary penances as have been recounted, that he led a life of what may be called unceasing mortification. He never allowed himself to sleep as nature prompted him. His bed was a plank and his pillow a faggot, but to lie on it undisturbed, even during the short time he allowed himself to sleep, was a luxury which he denied to his over-tired body. He knelt in prayer upon this so-called bed, till, overcome by drowsiness, he either rested on his elbow on the bundle of sticks, or else leaned against the wall for an hour or two. Always at work, always cheerful, it is a wonder that he was able to live through those forty years in Rome with only that brief snatch of sleep which he allowed himself while the friars sang their midnight office.

He never approached the fire except by obedience; yet he suffered acutely from cold. Sometimes on winter evenings, when he was chilled through, and his hands were too numb to do his work, he used to go into the garden and walk swiftly up and down. "What, ass," he would say, apostrophising himself, "do you pretend to be cold? Very well, then, it is all the more reason why you should be made to trot."

It was not only to mortify himself that he kept away from the stove, but also because he considered its comfort an occasion of sin. "Away from the fire!" he used to say. "It was while warming himself that Peter denied our Lord." He considered that any gathering round the stove was especially pernicious in a religious community, and a fruitful occasion of scandal and gossip. "Round the fire," he said to Brother Alessio, his frequent companion, "people talk a great deal too much; and such talk is sure to be idle, not at all to God's honour, and most likely to the injury of their neighbour." To point his moral he proceeded to relate to the brother an experience of his own.

"Last night," said he, "when I was in the church, the sanctuary lamp suddenly went out, and I hurried at once to the kitchen to fetch a candle. What did I see there but five brothers seated round the fire with their hands covered by their sleeves and their faces half hidden by their hoods. Looking at them intently, I recognised them. 'Why,' said I, 'you have been dead some time.

What are you doing here?' 'Alas, brother,' replied one of them, 'we have been sent back here by the justice of God until we have made satisfaction for our sins of the tongue, waste of time and idleness committed in this very place. Of your charity, Brother Felix, pray for us.' There, Brother Alessio, see what harm can befall a soul by warming the body, even if we feel great need of warmth. As for me, I would not mind dying of cold provided my heart were on fire with the love of God."

The suffering most joyfully accepted by the Saint was caused immediately by his special duties. The winter cold, the summer heat, the winds and wet to which he was exposed as he tramped about the streets of Rome, produced the most painful cracks and sores in his legs, inadequately covered as they were by his short, narrow habit. Far from doing anything to alleviate the pain, he pretended to cure the wounds in a manner which must have caused real torture, for he stitched them up with packthread, making holes for the purpose with a cobbler's awl. The state of his feet, chilled in winter and blistered in summer, and cut by the sharp stones and refuse with which the streets were littered, was terrible to behold. Sometimes each step he took caused him an agony which he could not altogether conceal, though it never made him flinch from his work. We have to remember this state of suffering when we picture to ourselves the Saint's weekly pilgrimage to the seven churches.

Far from only enduring his sufferings, he really loved them. On one occasion he was in a state of what many would have called agony, from internal inflammation brought on by exposure. The doctor, called in by the Father Guardian, did what he could to relieve him, but, trusting his patient's sanctity more than his own skill, he urged him to invoke the Holy Name, as he felt sure this would effect his cure. "What!" cried St. Felix indignantly, "you would have me invoke the Holy Name of Jesus in order to be delivered from suffering sent to me by God? I will do nothing of the sort. Do you not know that sufferings are the caresses which He lavishes on those whom He loves? Rather will I accept them from my heart with gratitude, and bear them for so long as He pleases."

Another time, when some one commiserated him for the acute pain he was undergoing, he replied that sufferings were the roses which grew in paradise, which God of His goodness distributes from time to time among His children. The only alleviation he allowed himself was singing sacred canticles. Often the pain fled before the holy and joyous song, and, seeing this, he recommended the same remedy, with the same effect, to the sick whom he was tending.

Much as St. Felix had to endure, he was not content with his own sufferings, but was envious if he heard of any one else being in pain. When one day visiting a cardinal—a benefactor of the convent—he found him confined to his bed with an excruciating attack of gout. "Oh, happy are you, Monsignor," he cried impulsively, "to be favoured with such sufferings! Would that I could change places with you!"

Hearing that a notorious criminal was—according to the custom of the age—to be tortured before he was put to death, he was filled with an unaffected desire to suffer in his stead. "Oh," he exclaimed, "why may I not bear this instead of him! God forbid that I should commit the crimes of which this is the penalty, but I would take his punishment with joy."

During the exorcism of one possessed, at which the Saint was present, he went so far as to offer his body to the devil to torment in whatever way he chose. It is recorded that, finding himself face to face with such devotion, the evil one left his victim, without daring to touch him who had offered himself in his stead.

Such was St. Felix's life—a life of continual mortification of nature, and of hard, ceaseless, thankless toil, carried on in the face of constant suffering. Yet it was by his sunny cheerfulness that he was best known to men. This need not surprise us, for the experience of centuries has made it into a truism, that those saints who have been most ruthless in their austerities have likewise been remarkable for their joyousness of heart and manner. St. Felix never flagged, and the happiness of his heart brimmed over into his speech. He could on occasion rebuke sin, even in high places, with unsparing severity, but as a rule he conveyed his rebukes with a shrewd, kindly, playful wit which carried his lesson home to the hearts of those to whom they were addressed.

He had promised to give Princess Colonna some of the little crosses, in making which he employed his spare moments. She asked him for them the next time that he went to beg at her palace, and he had to own that he had forgotten all about her request. It is evident that this great lady thought she had committed an act of condescension in asking for the gift, and her pride was injured by his forgetfulness, so that she reproached him haughtily. "I never heard of such a thing," said she, "as that a man like you should make me a promise, and not keep it." "Ah, Princess," replied St. Felix, "I know that I ought to have kept my word, but you must excuse me. Alas, it is but human infirmity. What a number of promises we make to God, and how seldom we keep them!"

He displayed the same readiness of wit in the way he met the advances of a Jew, who, prompted either by impertinence or by the desire to test the spirit of the holy brother about whom all Rome was talking, asked him to give him of his charity a morsel of bread from his wallet. "Ask for it in the name of Jesus Christ," replied the Saint, "and you shall have a whole loaf."

St. Felix had too great a regard for the law of charity to be willing to criticise freely, but when he was asked to pass judgment on anything which displeased him, he did so with a shrewd playfulness which removed the sting from the severe censure often conveyed by his words. Being unable to read, it was a great enjoyment to him to hear sermons, but he cordially disapproved of that grand kind of oratory prevalent before St. Philip introduced a simpler form of preaching. Being asked his opinion of a certain sermon of that description, he replied: "The preacher takes me back to my youth and reminds me of some peasants I once knew who sowed corn, but cared only for the production of fine tall straw which made people exclaim with wonder. They did not mind how poor the grain was."

Such was the man whose soul was formed and fed on austerities. Out of the abundance of the heart the mouth speaketh; and his joyous heart was so brimming over with habitual thankfulness that by degrees he became known throughout the city by no other name than that of Brother Deo-gratias, on account of his frequent use of the ejaculation. It was always on his lips, being on all occasions the spontaneous expression of his interior thought. He used it in joy, in sorrow, in sickness, in health, and the words filled his soul with such tenderness that when he had to pronounce them while serving Mass, tears filled his eyes and his voice failed him. His affection for the ejaculation dated back to his earlier days in Rome, when he had been deeply impressed by a sermon on it delivered by Father Alfonso Lupo, a famous preacher of his own Order. It so exactly supplied a want in his soul that he adopted it as a sort of watch-word. It was with it that he gave his blessing and returned salutations, with it that he reconciled enemies, and infused peace into the souls of the dying. Hearing him use the words so frequently, the little children in the streets, between whom and the Saint there always existed an affectionate intimacy, gave him the name of Brother Deo-gratias; and the name passed into general use.

CHAPTER V

THE NIGHTS WITH GOD

SUCH was St. Felix's life as others knew it. There was no one who could not perceive the joyous manner in which he accomplished his monotonous and arduous duties; and his brothers in religion could not but be aware of the heroic mortifications which he practised. It was patent to all men that he was year by year increasing in sanctity, but the prime cause of this spiritual growth was his own secret. Such, at least, the Saint intended it to be, and such it would have remained had it not been for the indiscretion of his admirers. Such indiscreet friends are, fortunately for posterity, always to be found on the track of the saints, making it their business to bring to light those things which the servants of God most wish to conceal, and handing down to future generations the record of shining acts which their authors would fain bury under a bushel.

To these friends do we owe the knowledge that St. Felix did not find rest from his labours in sleep, as did his equally toil-worn companions. He sought and found it in prayer alone; and in the strength of the spiritual refreshment thus obtained he was able to live out his long and arduous course without flagging.

As soon as the other friars had retired to their cells St. Felix went into the church. Solitude was a necessity to him, and his first business was to search diligently with the aid of a lighted candle, in case some fellow-worshipper should be concealed unbeknown to him. Not before he was sure of being alone would he give himself over to prayer. If he found any of the friars at their devotions he would do his best to persuade them to go to their cells, telling them that there was a time for all things, and

35

that they had better visit the Blessed Sacrament in the daytime; whereas he could not do so on account of his duties in the city. It was the Saint's undisguised desire to get rid of all fellow-worshippers which first induced his friends to watch him. What they saw from their places of concealment led them to repeat the experiment many times, with the result that they learned St. Felix's secret, and were able at the process for his beatification to testify on oath to the manner in which he passed his nights.

Having finished his investigations, and satisfied himself that he was, as he thought, alone, St. Felix extinguished his candle and trimmed the lamp before the altar most carefully. Then his first act was to take a severe discipline. So unsparing was he of himself that one and all of the hidden spies described with horror what they beheld. Father Lupo, the famous preacher, watched him frequently, and on one occasion, not being able to endure the sight, rushed from his place of concealment and seized the Saint's hand. "Brother, brother," he cried, "this is not chastising the body, it is killing it. Do you wish to be a self-murderer?"

"God forgive you, father," said St. Felix. "Why do you come here to pry into other people's concerns when you ought to be shut up in your cell?"

But still Lupo remonstrated with the brother for his over-severity. "What!" returned the Saint, "you would hinder me, who have offended God so deeply, from bewailing my offences? How else could I be content to live? Ah, rather than try to hinder me, you should pray to God to forgive me."

Sometimes St. Felix took the discipline not in the church but in an old vault where the first brothers of the reform were buried. There he used to apostrophise the dead, and on one occasion was heard to speak thus, weeping the while: "Oh you, my brethren, you whose lives were one long penance, I will speak to you. You were no cowards; you fought generously and finished your course gloriously. You warred against the flesh and kept your bodies in subjection; and now, having fought the good fight, you have gone to receive your crown at the hands of a just judge!"

It was not often that the watchers' patience was rewarded by the sight of anything extraordinary in their holy companion's converse with the unseen world. The long hours of the night were usually spent in that ordinary prayer, in which he sought his refreshment; and as soon as he found himself undisturbed in the presence of God he put into simple words the thoughts that arose within him. At all times he preferred to talk from his heart in prayer; and though most precise in his recitation of the rosary and other vocal prayers prescribed to lay-brothers by the rule, he did not usually have recourse to *Paters* and *Aves* in his intercourse with heaven. Indeed, the repetition aloud of vocal prayers by others rather annoyed him. "Know, brother," said he to his companion who was muttering *Aves* audibly as he walked along, "know that the voice of the heart is more agreeable to God than that of the lips, and would do you more good."

Most, therefore, of the prayers overheard by the watchers were conversational outpourings either to our Lord or his blessed Mother. He would also often address his holy father, St. Francis, to whom he would stretch out his arms as if he beheld him with his eyes. "Oh, my father," he would say, "your poor Brother Felix commends himself to your care. Remember that he is your son, and that, however unworthy he may be, he loves you with all his heart. Help me, dear Father, and direct all the actions of my life. Do not leave me till you have brought me to the feet of Jesus, whom you loved so much when you were on earth."

Many of St. Felix's conversational prayers were of petition, and frequently took the form of intercession for benefactors. "O Lord God!" he said in one prayer recorded, "Jesus, full of goodness and mercy, I commend all these people to Thee. Look after all the good men and women, who for love of Thee heap benefits on us day after day, and feed Thy poor ones. Give them grace for grace and gift for gift." Another time, during a season of general distress caused by incessant rain, the Saint was overheard to pray long and earnestly for relief. "Lord," said he, "Thy mercy makes me bold. I declare to Thee that I will not leave Thee until this rain ceases!" Thus did he pray, and it is recorded by a witness that the state of the weather improved from that night.

Often St. Felix's thoughts found expression in the Psalms and Antiphons of the Divine Office, heard by him when sung by the friars in choir. He had a wonderfully retentive memory, and stored up what he heard for future use. When not sure of either the wording or meaning of a passage, he used to seek out one of the fathers and ask him for an explanation, and would repeat the part over and over again till he was sure of it.

His joyous mind was full of song; and not only did he sing the Antiphons and Psalms which he had learnt, but also verses which he had composed himself. These verses or rhymes, roughly strung together, were full of fervour, but innocent of all laws of versification. The following is a specimen of these rough verses:

> Gesù dolce mio sposo
> Fonte del divin' amore
> Me scrivesti nel cuore
> Che io ti dovessi amare
> Signore, tu me creasti
> Perche io te amassi.

Another, addressed to our Lady, ran thus:

> In questa terra è nata una rosella
> O quant' è bella, quant' è bella
> Maria verginella.

The following lines have a special interest as being used by the Saint himself as a panacea against suffering, and recommended to others in pain and sickness as a sure remedy:

> Chi la croce stringe bene
> Gesù Cristo te soviene
> E il paradis' ottiene.

"Press the cross with love," he would add, in explanation of the verses. "Press it as hard as you can, and your trouble will be changed to delight."

The habit of composing them began when he was keeping sheep as a boy, and was continued by him all through life. In them he expressed his emotions and desires of the time being, and, having set them to airs as crude as the words, he recommended them to his friends to sing, which they gladly did, till by degrees the verses passed into general use throughout Rome.

True son of St. Francis, he had a tender devotion to the Holy Infancy—a devotion which he did his utmost to promote. Before Christmas he used to go round to the houses of his richer acquaintances, and say, "Have you prepared a room for your expected guest?" And when they, being, or feigning to be astonished, asked to whom he referred, he would reply, "Why, who else could it be but that great Lady, who is about to give birth to the Saviour? Make haste and prepare a room where she and her Son may dwell."

It was remarked that as Christmas approached the constant subject of the Saint's prayer were the words, *Et Verbum caro factum est*, which he would repeat over and over again. Being, as he said them, apparently lost to the things of sense, he went through the motions of clasping the Divine Infant in his arms. At other times he would in a similar manner repeat the Holy Name again and again in different cadences, for many minutes together.

But the theme of most of St. Felix's meditations was the Sacred Passion. Sometimes it seemed to the watchers as if he were acting it to himself as a drama, by repeating the narrative in the words of Scripture, and showing by his actions his detestation of Judas and his indignation with the faithless apostles, or manifesting his compassion for our Lord's sufferings and the sorrows of Mary. "What, Lord Jesus," he was heard to cry out, "Thou wert alone—abandoned by Thy disciples—with no one to defend Thee? Oh, where was I then?"

When questioned about his prayer, and how it was that he could find so much food for meditation without being able to glean thoughts from spiritual books, the Saint replied that he was possessed of a breviary which consisted of six letters, five being red and one white, namely, the five sacred wounds of our blessed Lord, and the holy Mother of God. "If," added he, "I had the grace to understand these six letters perfectly, I would not yield to any

doctor or theologian of the first rank. Pray to God and his holy
Mother that I may understand better."

He usually prayed aloud, but at times his voice sank into
silence, and he remained speechless and motionless in prayer for
hours at a time. So motionless was he that the watcher, losing
patience, would go and shake him to bring him back to his
senses; and the Saint, recalled to himself, would gently complain
of the interruption.

Such is a portion of what has been recorded by the persever-
ing watchers as the result of their observations. They saw much,
but there was more that they did not see; for we may assume that
their vigilance was but partial, and that much that took place
between Felix and the unseen world must have been unobserved
by human eye. When, however, we consider the assiduity of
these spies, it stands to reason that such hard-worked men would
not have deprived themselves of their natural rest, had nothing
save the sight of their holy brother in fervent though ordinary
prayer, such as has been described, rewarded their perseverance.
They would never have persisted in their observations had they
not thereby obtained some glimpses behind the veil.

It was evident to all beholders that sometimes when St. Felix
spoke to our Lord he saw with his eyes that which it was not
given to the watchers to see. His look was fixed, to the exclusion
of all else, on some object before him; and had those concealed
been bold enough to disturb him at such times, he would most
probably have been unaware of their presence. "Ah, Jesus, my
Love," he was heard to cry aloud; "do not go from me. I am
coming; wait for me!" And as he spoke he ran towards the altar,
borne along, as it seemed, by unseen hands, until, when close to
the tabernacle, he was raised from the ground, and remained
suspended in the air rapt in prayer. Several times was this marvel
seen by the watchers, who bore testimony on oath to what they
had witnessed.

This was not all, for on some few occasions the eyes of the
hidden friars were opened to see also the things which their
brother saw. One night, as St. Felix knelt in prayer on the altar
step, as close as he could approach to the Blessed Sacrament, two

of the watchers beheld our Lord appear under the form of an Infant, surrounded by an indescribable light, before whom the Saint threw himself on his face in silent adoration. Then, as if obeying some call unheard by the watchers, he rose to his feet, and, taking the Divine Child in his arms, embraced Him—and then the vision melted from the observers' sight.

How often this divine intercourse was held between Felix and his Lord, when no one else was present, must remain the Saint's own secret; but once again, near Christmas, the same marvellously beautiful vision was beheld. This night Fra Lupo and another were concealed, and they heard the servant of God implore our Lady to show him her Child once more. As he prayed she appeared holding in her arms the Divine Infant, whom she placed in those of Felix. The Saint clasped Him, and for some moments held conversation with Him, in which the Child seemed to answer. Then, having by command embraced the Infant, he placed Him back in His Mother's arms, and the watchers saw no more.

Thus passed those wondrous nights which explain how it was that labour and fasting, wounds and weariness were as nothing to the Saint. It was his duty to ring the bell for Matins which were sung at midnight. While the friars were in choir, St. Felix went to his cell and snatched those moments of sleep which he allowed himself to take, under the circumstances already related. He remained in his cell during that time with mind at ease, because, as he said, our Lord was no longer alone in the church.

Thither, however, he returned when the friars had finished their Office, and occupied himself in the same manner as during the earlier portion of the night. Thus he remained till the hour of Prime, when he began the daily round of his life by hearing Mass. His careful weekly Communion, which as a working-man he had never neglected to make, had, when he entered religion, given way first to two and then to three Communions a week, until during the latter portion of his life he received the bread of life every day. After his Communion he heard and served as many Masses as he could before the time for beginning his rounds arrived. Thus he went on day by day, year by year, leading a life with no variation, hearing Mass till he went begging, begging till night came on, and praying till morning dawned, drawing ever nearer and nearer to God by means of this holy monotony.

CHAPTER VI

FRATERNAL CORRECTION

HE veneration in which St. Felix was held by his own Community can be inferred by the pains taken by his brothers in religion to watch and record his movements. Though, had he suspected any such sentiment, he would have indignantly repudiated all claim on their admiration, he could not but be aware of the very responsible position which he, a simple and uneducated lay-brother, held in the convent. That he knew it, was betrayed by his readiness with advice, and even censure, when he felt them to be required.

He was frequent in his exhortations to absolute detachment from home ties, for, said he, all Friars Minor should imitate St. Francis, who would own no father on earth. To those who were apt to worry themselves about the temporal affairs of their relatives in the world, he would quote in warning our Lord's words, "He that putteth his hand to the plough and looketh back is not fit for the kingdom of heaven," a simile the force of which must have been obvious to himself.

"Alas, poor father," he said to one of the Community who owned to him that he had arranged to visit his family on the plea of business, and begged of the Saint some of his little crosses to take home as gifts; "how much you are to be pitied if you can give the name of relatives to those whom you renounced so long ago. They were so once, but since you gave up your home they belong to you no longer, and they should be to you as though they were strangers. Beware, father; take my advice and do not carry out your purpose of visiting them. Pray for them, and by so doing you will help them more than by a hundred visits."

43

One of the Community, knowing the power of the Saint's influence in high places, asked him to use it to obtain some favour for one of his relatives. "No, father," he replied, "I cannot do such a thing. In this matter you would do well to follow the example of ignorant old Brother Felix, and let the dead bury their dead."

He might safely appeal to his own example, for from the day when he distributed his goods among the poor to the exclusion of his own family, there is no record that he had any further communication with his relatives. No doubt he was mindful of their spiritual interests, and watched over them from heaven as well as on earth, as is indeed proved by the story of young Marco's death. But though he would own no kin, he could not divest himself of a sense of responsibility towards his native home; and the only incident which connects him in later life with Cantalice is illustrative of his care for its spiritual needs.

It is evident that the dissensions which were an element of discord in his memories of childhood, and which still prevailed in the village, filled him with pain and anxiety even after he had severed his connection with the scenes of his youth. To remedy the evil he turned to account that influence in high places which he had refused to use for the temporal benefit of his companion's relatives, and obtained from Gregory XIII the grant of a plenary indulgence especially applicable to his former fellow-villagers. The condition for gaining the indulgence was the relinquishment of feuds and quarrels, with the adoption of a peaceable mode of life. This local privilege, the terms of which are unique, gives us an idea of the great influence of him who succeeded in obtaining it.

The bull having been received by the Capuchins, St. Felix was charged by his superiors to convey it to his old home. He would not dwell within the precincts of the village, but passed the night in a cottage among the hills, belonging to one of his brothers; and there he wrought a miracle which is especially worthy of notice as being the first instance mentioned of the supernatural dominion exercised by him over articles of food, which is such a marked feature in the miracles wrought by him in later years.

The Saint's brother regarded Felix's sojourn under his roof as the greatest of honours, and the wife was anxious to offer him and his companion fitting hospitality. "Put yourself to no trouble on our account," said St. Felix, perceiving the preparations which the good woman was making for his supper. "We want nothing but a few boiled beans, which you had better go and gather in the garden."

Had her brother-in-law expressed a desire for nightingales' tongues the poor woman could not have felt more embarrassed, and she reminded him with confusion that he must have forgotten the season, for that beans were not as yet even in flower. "You are mistaken," he replied coldly; "go and look." Still his sister-in-law continued to argue the point. "Do not be obstinate," he then said sharply. "Is not God all-powerful? Go and do as I tell you." Being ashamed of making further resistance, the good woman, to humour her guest, went into the garden, where, to her surprise, she found some ripe beans, sufficient to make a dish.

Having given supper to the friars, the hostess busied herself with the preparation of their bed-chamber, and produced her best linen. In this, however, she carried her hospitality too far, and without either protest or explanation, St. Felix and his companion left the house, and, in spite of all remonstrances, passed the night under a tree. Next morning, having handed over the documents he had brought to the parish priest, the Saint returned to Rome without paying a single visit or exchanging a word with any one in Cantalice.

St. Felix's great influence over his own brothers in religion arose from the sense of responsibility for their spiritual welfare, which, though he was only a lay-brother and a most unlearned man, governed all his dealings with them from the beginning of his life in Rome. As was natural, it was towards the other lay-brothers that it first manifested itself, and it led him frequently to make them the objects of severe fraternal correction. It may be remembered how he himself avoided the fireside as an occasion of sin, and how he warned Brother Alessio against it; but he went further than this. If he saw any of the brothers warming themselves at the stove and talking idly, he went up to the group, and if they did not at once disperse, he would stand by and seem to be interested in the conversation. Then, during a pause, he would perhaps say: "Oh, pardon me, I thought you were speaking about spiritual matters or I would not have listened. Good-bye, and pray for me."

He was more severe if he perceived among them any symptoms of what he considered gluttony. There were some in the Community who even in those days of fervour were discontented with the coarse and common food served out to them, and who accepted, and even sought for, greater delicacies from their friends outside. "Oh," the Saint said reproachfully to such as these, "why do you profess to be poor religious if you hanker after the luxuries of the rich? How can you take so much trouble to fatten a body which will ere long be food for worms?"

St. Felix's love for the young, which was a marked characteristic of his child-like soul, made him take a special interest in the youths—often mere lads—who came in numbers to ask to follow Christ along the rough paths of the Capuchin reform. "Santarelli," he would say, addressing them by the name he usually bestowed on little children, "now is your time. Practise mortifications most carefully now during your novitiate, for habits of virtue as well as of vice formed in early years last even to old age, and will accompany you to the grave."

One of these young men, though zealous and observant, was so profoundly melancholy that all could see that he had some secret trouble on his soul. It was to the old lay-brother that he at last opened his heart, and confided to him that when he was in the world, being ruined by a course of gambling, he had, in a moment of despair, given himself to the devil, and had even signed a written compact to that effect. This bargain had, it is true, proved no obstacle to either his conversion or religious vocation; but, since he had been in the convent, the devil had left him no peace, and appeared constantly to him, maltreated him, and claimed him as his own. St. Felix was at first so horrified by the idea of a Christian making such a compact, that he added to the young man's sufferings by upbraiding him; but seeing that he was driving him to despair, he consoled him by pointing out that, as he had withdrawn the gift, the evil one had no further claim on him. This was not enough; but by prayer and sympathy, and by keeping near the young man during his fits of diabolic despair, which drove him to seek his own life, the Saint by degrees overcame the enemy, who withdrew and suffered the novice to make his profession, and live and die in the service of God.

Nothing that took place in the Community escaped the observation of the unlettered old Saint. He had a great veneration for learning, but his soul was grieved if he saw any of the friars devote more time to study than to prayer, which he considered to be contrary to the spirit of St. Francis. He, as usual, spoke his mind and spared none. He told the great preachers of the Order who, as in the case of Fra Lupo, were renowned throughout Italy, that by prayer alone could the disciples of the cross learn how to preach. Nor did he confine such inculcations to his own brethren.

There was a learned theologian, Andrea Montino, who devoted his time and talents to refuting the errors of the Jews, without, apparently, succeeding in making many conversions. St. Felix found him one day in his library busily preparing a lecture, and told him bluntly that he was wasting his time. "If you wish to convert these obstinate people," said he, "it is useless to wear yourself out with study, which is to no purpose. Let me give you a piece of advice, and if you take it you will find your lectures much more effective. I am, remember, a poor, ignorant old man, but this is my advice. Study your crucifix, for there you will find the whole teaching of God." "You are right," cried Andrea. "Your words are the words of God." Then, lifting up his voice, the theologian humbly thanked God for revealing His secrets to those who owe nothing to human learning.

So great was the respect in the Community for the Saint's opinion, and so timid were the friars of his censure of any departure from the rule, especially in the matter of poverty, that they often allowed themselves to be entirely influenced by such fear. The superiors were known to neglect even necessary repairs to the buildings lest they should lay themselves open to rebuke from the old lay-brother.

One anecdote is related which, while it makes known the Saint's gift of reading the thoughts of men, is still more illustrative of the high position he held in the Order. Father Santi, the Vicar-provincial of the Capuchins, who lived in Rome, having remarked that some time had elapsed since St. Felix had sought him out to consult him and converse about spiritual matters, as was his wont, grew low-spirited. His depression was caused by a conviction that the Saint had discovered in him some secret sin, of which he was himself unaware, and was avoiding him from detestation of it. But the old lay-brother's absence had been accidental, and one evening, while Father Santi was morbidly brooding over his grievance, St. Felix walked into his room, and, though throwing more than usual respect into his manner, gave him two playful taps on the cheek, and then went away, leaving the Provincial full of consolation. He was convinced that his anxiety of mind had been made known supernaturally to the servant of God, who had taken this means to assure him of his affection and esteem.

Human respect never held back the Saint from administering reproof where he felt it to be needed; but in no case did he show more moral courage than when he rebuked priests; for one of his most marked characteristics was veneration for the sacerdotal state. Yet he could be severe in his censures even in their case, especially if he saw one saying Mass carelessly or hurriedly. He would take him aside at a convenient opportunity and point the lesson conveyed by the extreme deliberation with which our Lord instituted the Holy Eucharist, so that though He "desired with desire" to give Himself to His disciples, He put off doing so till the end of His life, and would not advance the day or hour He had fixed.

So great was St. Felix's reverence for priests that, wherever he met one, he could not be restrained from asking his blessing on his knees. Nothing wounded him more than having such a request refused. One day he thus knelt and asked the blessing of two Jesuit fathers whom he met near the church of St Sebastian; but they, pleading their unworthiness, refused it and begged him to rise. "My holy father St. Francis regarded all priests as his superiors," replied the Saint reproachfully. "Would you prevent me from proving myself to be his son by following his example, and doing that which he enjoined on us to do?"

As years went by St. Felix was held in such veneration that, wherever he appeared, people crowded round him to kiss his hand. These manifestations of respect were always painful, and he tried to avoid them by covering his hand with his habit which he presented to them to kiss, for thus, said he, they bestowed their marks of reverence not on him but on the livery of his holy father. If, however, he found himself in the company of a priest when the populace showed their devotion in this way, his horror of the honour paid him was too great for endurance. Drawing the priest forward he would with confusion call on the people to bestow their veneration on him instead, on account of his sacerdotal state.

Still greater was his reverence for bishops; and an anecdote of the manner in which he proved it on one occasion furnishes a graphic picture of the circumstances of the Saint's life. One day, the city being flooded by an inundation of the Tiber, he was threading his way along a narrow causeway which had been constructed for foot-passengers in the Via Lata—as the Corso was then called—when he saw a Bishop approaching from the opposite end. Naturally, he stepped back to let the other cross first; but the Bishop had as high a regard for the begging-brother's sanctity as the latter had for his office, and wished to wait his turn and let the Capuchin cross first. Seeing his hesitation, St. Felix promptly jumped off the causeway into the water, which reached above his knees. "God forgive you," cried the Bishop, "what have you done?"—"Why," replied the Saint, "I have but done what a laden ass should do. Pray give me your blessing."

When the occasion offered, St. Felix was ready to extend his fraternal correction to those in the very highest places, though never so ready to do so as at the call of obedience. At one time the Capuchins suffered much trouble at the hands of their

Protector, Cardinal Santorio, who, while devoted to them and their interests, took too much upon him, encouraged the complaints of malcontents, and even went so far as to cancel the commands of their lawful superiors. The only man whom the Community considered to be capable of applying a remedy to this displeasing state of things was Felix the lay-brother; and he, when sent to remonstrate with the Cardinal, did so without hesitancy or human respect.

"We all know, Monsignor," he said, when admitted with his companion to the Cardinal's presence, "that our Order has been put under your protection; and that His Holiness has commended it very specially to your care. But he did this in order that you might defend it, not that you might destroy it by the misuse of your authority. We complain that you refuse to admit our superiors to an audience, while any of the religious who are dissatisfied with their rule receive free permission to speak to you. There is nothing connected with our government that you do not take upon yourself; you impose commands on some, you grant exemptions to others; you appoint commissioners without notice; you suppress chapters; you postpone them; you annul elections, and, in short, you overset everything. We know that your intention is good, and we are persuaded that you are unaware how much harm you are doing. So I pray you to forgive my boldness and take in good part this counsel which I, a poor lay-brother, venture to give you. Do not interfere any more with the internal government of our houses. That is the business of our superiors, yours is to protect them. They are charged with the care of their subjects, and will have to render an account of their office to God. Your duty is to uphold them in this great charge."

The Saint's companion was terrified when he heard these bold words; but he need not have feared. The Cardinal was much struck by the speech of the unlettered brother, and never again did the Capuchins have the same cause for complaint.

CHAPTER VII

ST. FELIX'S APOSTOLATE

THOUGH the power of St. Felix's influence over men began in his own convent, it was far from ending there, and soon spread throughout Rome. So widespread was his spiritual empire that as we study his life we seem to be following the steps of one whose vocation it was to be an apostle only, and we might forget that his ostensible work in life was to provide food for a religious community which lived on alms, and that the conversion of souls was extraneous to his state. It is difficult to know exactly when his work as a collector of alms began to take the form of an apostolate, or whether he were in reality an apostle even before he shouldered a wallet. It is, in fact, almost impossible to trace the exact beginning of any of the changes which mark St. Felix's career. Even as, in the holy monotony of his life, the evening and the morning of his days were indistinguishable, so was it with his whole earthly pilgrimage. All his actions, motives, and feelings belong equally to middle life and old age, there being no salient epoch discoverable in any one of the forty years during which he tramped about the streets of Rome.

God's ways of working through His creatures are full of surprises, but few in the whole history of the Church are more startling or conducive to thought than the influence of St. Felix over the minds of men, and the share taken by him in the renovation of Christianity in Rome. To have influenced Rome means that he influenced the world, for she in those days was its leader, not only as the See of Peter, but as the centre of learning and civilisation. There, in the middle of the sixteenth

51

century, society was only recovering—not yet recovered—from the unchristianising effects of the pagan renaissance. Though the worship of paganism was no longer rampant, the love of erudition for erudition's sake which it had conjured up remained, and placed the Eternal City at that time in the van of the intellectual movement which marked the age. Here, then, it was, in the capital of the world, and in a century of pride and independence, that God saw fit to raise up one of those divinely foolish things with which He is wont to confound the wise.

That where sin abounds grace does much more abound has become a truism to those who have even a cursory knowledge of the history of the Church; and nowhere is the truth of St. Paul's words more patent than in the story of the sixteenth century. Almost the same years which saw the birth of the heresiarchs of that age of rebellion and license saw that of some of the greatest saints ever put into the world by God to counteract evil. They grew up side by side like the wheat and the cockle, their true character unknown and unperceived till the hour of God came. All this is known to readers of Church history, to those outside the fold as well as to those within, although with the former there may exist some confusion as to who was on God's side and who on Satan's.

The Saints came forth in cohorts, drawn from all countries and all classes—St. Philip and St. Charles, St. Ignatius and St. Francis Xavier, St. Theresa and St. Catherine of Genoa, St. John of the Cross and St. Peter of Alcantara, and too many more to enumerate. One and all stepped forth to do God's work, at God's time and in His own way, being marvellously fitted for the special post they were called on to fill, and astounding the world by their power. Among this rich harvest of Saints grew up our humble St. Felix; and the tremendous influence of this poor untaught farm-labourer is, we venture to think, one of the most startling manifestations of God's ways with men.

When His glory and the salvation of souls are at stake, class distinctions become as nothing in the hands of God. Rich and poor, learned and ignorant, prince and peasant, are used indiscriminately in His service; and when the occasion arises He moves His creatures to ignore lesser differences, and—seeing as He sees—to distinguish man from man solely by the light of divine judgment. Every democratic sentiment produced by this or any other century has been, in a sense, outdone in the history of the Church, founded by our Lord on an unlettered fisherman. In the annals of the Saints, and—what is more to the purpose— especially in that grand group who renovated Christianity in the sixteenth century, we find all classes represented. We shall, however, find none lower in the social scale than Felix, first peasant, then ploughman, and lastly lay-brother, ignorant of the very elements of learning, unpolished in manner and rough in speech to the very end of his life.

Such a man as he might, without disrespect, be supposed to have found himself more at home in a kitchen or barn than in the banqueting-halls and drawing-rooms of a fastidious and cultivated society; yet we find him as welcome a guest and as much at home in the houses of the rich as in those of the poor. His exterior disadvantages and want of polish were forgotten in his sanctity, and it never occurred to him to feel out of place where souls were to be won to God. We find him consoling Cardinals on their sick-beds, teaching judges the laws of justice, and physicians the art of healing; or again, we find him by the bedside of the highest ladies of the land, blessing the birth of their new-born babes, or, in other cases, comforting them in their last moments.

There is one incident in St. Felix's life essentially descriptive of the so-called incongruity of his position in Roman society, which could not have occurred save in a Christian city and Christian age. Many among the benefactors of whom he begged, craved what they considered the honour of his presence at their tables; but each invitation of the kind was met by an unequivocal refusal. There was one among them, the owner of a palace, who desired so much to entertain him at a banquet, that, by dint of perseverance, he persuaded the Saint's superiors to command him to accept the invitation. As the holy brother sat at the table, which seemed to him to groan under its weight of luxuries, he grew each moment more miserable. He turned in a bewildered

manner to one of his fellow guests after the other, and asked
what such a mode of repast could mean. At last, losing his self-
control, he stretched out his arms, and uttered a wild appeal to
be delivered from the horrible position in which he found
himself. Scarcely less remarkable, from a descriptive point of
view, is the account of his visits to the drawing-rooms of the
wealthy, where, surrounded by the admiring members of the
family, he would stand, shouting out his sacred verses to the top
of his voice, accompanied on their spinet by young lady-
musicians.

To fully appreciate such a scene, it is necessary to draw a
mental sketch of the Saint's personal appearance. We must
picture him as he was when thus made the centre of an admiring
group, and try to see him with the eyes of those in the midst of
whom he stood, with his back bowed under the weight of wallet
and gourds and their heterogeneous contents, and clad in his
skimpy, patched and very dirty habit which could not conceal his
scarred and seamed legs, or his cut, bruised feet, soiled with the
mire of the streets. There is, moreover, a further aspect of the
Saint's exterior, which, not only would it be dishonest to ignore,
but omission of which in any portrait of him would destroy some
of the admiration with which we must regard his influence on
Roman society.

Catholic writers have protested indignantly against the
accusation that dirt is regarded by the Church as a note of
sanctity, and have satisfactorily proved the contrary. Nevertheless, some individual saints, moved by we know not what thirst
for humiliation and mortification, have undoubtedly thus
regarded it. With St. Felix, his unwashed condition was the result
neither of indifference nor simplicity, nor did it arise from a
desire to mortify himself by a disregard for either comfort or
appearances; for we know from himself that he regarded dirt as
in itself a holy state. Those who loved him best were aware that
he would be improved—at least in the eyes of the world—by the
application of a little soap and water; and with this object in view
some of his young friends, the light-hearted German students,
laid a plot against him. They came on the old Saint by surprise,

and while some held him down, the others gave him a thorough washing. He bore the treatment with his habitual good humour, but afterwards gravely protested to his tormentors that they had robbed him of his chief ornament, which he speedily did his best to recover.

The influential position held by St. Felix in Roman society was of gradual growth, though, like everything else, it must have a beginning. As far as such a thing can be discovered in the Saint's unvarying life, we trace the germ of his apostolate in his intercourse with little children. These were especially dear to him on account of their own innocence, and as the reflection of Him to whose Holy Infancy he was so devout. His child-like soul expanded in their company, and they regarded him as their especial property. It was they who, as has been related, took up the Saint's favourite ejaculation, and, applying it to himself, called him Brother Deo-gratias, shouting out the words with glee whenever they caught sight of him. Then he, taking up their cry, and turning it into music of his own fashion, would gather the little ones around him and make them join with him in singing these and other holy words, till they were all tired.

The Saint's own so-called canticles took a large part in his apostolate, and were adopted everywhere. Young ladies set them to music and sang them with their harpsichords, and the sick and dying repeated them with a fervour which never failed to bring relief; but with none were they so popular as with the children who ran about the streets of Rome. We can almost see these little ones clustering round their dear old Brother Deo-gratias, clamouring, and vying with each other who should kiss his hand and habit. Having reduced them to some sort of order, he would arrange them in a circle, and, standing in their midst, would make them join with him in the well-known verses, beating time with his big stick. "Louder, santarelli," he would say, "sing all together, louder, louder." Then, moved by the sound of the shrill voices singing the divine praises, and unable to conceal his emotion, he would stop the performance. "Go away now, santarelli," he would say. "We will sing again another time with just the same words, but mind—and do not forget—we must sing louder and louder still."

It was not only the poorer children playing about the streets who regarded St. Felix as their property. As soon as he appeared, wallet on back, to beg for alms at the houses of the wealthy, the children within used to run to the door, and, some seizing him by his cord and others by his hand, they would drag him joyfully to a room where there was a musical instrument, and beg him to sing his verses with them. Every incident in St. Felix's life which reveals the manner of his intercourse with children has a special charm of its own. Even his supernatural gifts, such as prophecy and miracles, when exercised on their behalf have a distinctive beauty belonging to them.

His business took him one day through a schoolroom where a number of little boys were at their lessons. As soon as he appeared the children crowded round him to kiss his hand and obtain his blessing. After he had, as was his wont, made them sing with him, and when silence was restored, the Saint looked fixedly at a little boy named Giulio, and, putting his arm round him, drew him apart. "Oh, happy child," said he with tears in his eyes, "would that I were worthy to receive the happiness which will soon be yours!" And full of emotion he pressed him to his heart. Seeing the child's look of surprised inquiry, he went on: "I have such good news for you, Giulio santarello. In three days the angels will come to fetch you. Say *Deo gratias, Deo gratias*, my son, and when you are in heaven, pray for me."

When school was over, Giulio ran home full of glee, add told the good news to his parents. "In three days," he cried joyfully, "I am going to heaven with the angels. Brother Felix told me." The child's mother did not consider this good news, and to prove that she attached no importance to the announcement, she boxed Giulio's ears in her annoyance, and bade him not talk nonsense. "But you cannot prevent my going," replied the child merrily. Next day the happy little boy sickened with fever, and on the third day, true to the Saint's promise, the angels came to fetch him.

St. Felix was always quick to see signs of death in the little ones he loved so well, and rejoiced when God took them to Himself in a state of baptismal innocence. A lady of his acquaintance sent for him to show him her firstborn son, then a few days old, and obtain his blessing. "Paradise, little innocent, paradise," said he, taking the baby in his arms and looking lovingly at him. "You must get ready to go to heaven, little one." "I hope he will go there," replied the young mother, "but not till he is a very old man." "Nay," said the Saint, "soon, very soon. Do not try to keep him; let him go and take his place among the angels."

It was probably the same childlike purity and simplicity which drew the hearts of children to him that gave him a rare ascendency over animals, such as was exercised by his holy father, St. Francis. A horse had been tied up in a by-street, and while pawing the ground had caught its hoof in the grating of a cellar window. The poor beast was nearly mad with terror, and plunged so violently that no one dared approach to set it free, and every one felt sure that it must break its leg in its struggles. Just then St. Felix passed by and learned the state of affairs. "Stop, stop," he said to the bystanders who were rushing about, nearly as wild in their terror as the horse, "it is all right. Let me manage it." So saying, he went up to the animal, threw his cloak over its head, and put his arm round its neck. The poor beast stood perfectly still until an armourer was fetched from a distance to file the grating and free the hoof.

All creatures loved St. Felix, and as he walked about the lanes in the suburbs, or worked in the convent garden, the birds used to flock around him, settle on his shoulders, and even creep into his beard and peck his lips. He used to talk to them and feed them with morsels of bread, and they would never leave him until he himself dismissed them.

CHAPTER VIII

REBUKE OF SIN

ITH the expansion of St. Felix's sphere of influence his knowledge of sin and sinners received great increase. It was a foregone conclusion that he, who almost as an infant rebuked evil in his little companions, would not hold his peace now when he found himself in contact with sins far more grievous than he ever dreamt of as existing when he dwelt among the villages and mountains of the Abruzzi. It soon became known that the simple and joyous brother, who won little children and even the birds and beasts by his gentleness, could be unsparing enough in his rebukes when he saw or heard anything that was displeasing to God. What is more, all, men and women, rich and poor, feared the reproaches of the unlettered lay-brother, and amended their ways at his bidding.

Like all saints whose lot is cast in Catholic countries St. Felix was grieved to the soul by the vice and license which prevailed during the time of carnival. His brother in religion, Fra Lupo, having been compelled to pass through the riotous crowd on one such occasion, was so affected and horror-struck by the disorders he beheld, that he went at once to find St. Felix and obtain his help. He poured out to him his sorrow and indignation, and consulted with him what could be done to prevent, as he said, "our Lord being thus crucified afresh." It is characteristic of the humble lay-brother's position in the Community that it should have been with him that Lupo took counsel. Together the two Capuchins, the famous preacher and the begging-brother, organised a procession which at the time created no small sensation, and for that year at least effected the desired end.

It is in connection with this procession that we find Felix's name linked for the first time with that of St. Philip, whose apostolate in Rome extended through all the years that St. Felix went begging about the city. They must have been known to each other long before this procession was thought of, for the business of both Saints took them a great deal about the streets. It is almost safe to say that, though the intercourse of the two Saints is commemorated by only a few anecdotes, scarcely a week could have passed, during a large portion of their lives, without a chance meeting between them.

St. Philip, who once said of Felix that he was the greatest saint the world possessed, was consulted by the Capuchins, and gladly fell into their project by sending some of his fathers to head the procession with a large crucifix and lighted tapers. The sons of St. Francis followed, bearing in their hands skulls and other reminders of death. Last of all came St. Felix leading Fra Lupo—on whose lips all Rome hung—by a cord round his neck, intended to be a living representation, which none of the revellers could fail to understand, of our Lord being led to His judgment and death. This strange procession wended its way right through the midst of the masqueraders; and when the attention of the crowd had been thoroughly aroused, Fra Lupo lifted up his voice and preached fervently about sin and hell. At the end of the sermon the throng dispersed, and, for that season, no further scandals resulted from the merry-making.

While ostensibly occupied in collecting alms, St. Felix was ever on the look-out for opportunities of preventing sin. If he found young men hovering near haunts of vice, he spoke warningly to them, whether he knew them or not. "My son," said he to one such stranger, "do not run to your ruin. You are standing on the brink of a precipice, one step and it is all over with you. Do not forget that you have to die."

He was as outspoken when it was the benefactors of his convent who transgressed the law of God; for he never allowed the fear of losing their alms to restrain his tongue. There was a lady who was lavish with her charity, but who dressed with a want of modesty which Felix's zeal for souls would not allow him to pass unnoticed. Having one day given him a generous alms, she kept the Saint standing at the door, talking to him and trying to draw him into a conversation on spiritual matters; but not by one word would he respond to her pious sentiments. At last, affronted by the implied contempt, she took him sharply to task and demanded the reason of his silence. He, in reply, begged her to excuse him, as he feared to offend her by an explanation. When, however, she insisted, he preached her such a severe lesson on the subject of modesty, that, filled with confusion, she burst into tears. But she made noble reparation for her fault. "May your mouth be ever blessed, O servant of God," she exclaimed, "whence have this day proceeded words of life. Never again, I promise you, will I transgress in this way."

It was not always that he received such a generous response to his outspoken home-truths. There was another lady of high position who led a notoriously scandalous life. Time after time did St. Felix visit her, upbraid her, and threaten her with divine punishments, till, though she obstinately refused to hearken to his words, she conceived a great veneration for him personally. One day, impelled by this sentimental devotion to him, she sent to ask him for some vegetables out of his wallet, wherewith to make a salad. At this request the Saint lost patience, and sent back word by her messenger that not only should she receive nothing from him, but that she should never see his face again. He kept his word, though, shortly after, he sent her a final message to the effect that he still prayed for her, but that she had better beware, as he knew she would die ere long.

No one was safe from St. Felix's keen observation and shrewd rebukes. A judge, named Bernardine Biscia, was held in high repute for his learning, though he was not as famous for the justice of his decisions. St. Felix, wallet on back, visited this man in his private office, which was littered with books of reference and files of papers.

"Signor," said the Saint, tapping the books, "what is the use of all these things?" "Ah, Brother Felix," replied the judge good-naturedly, "there lie all the secrets of my profession. There I learn the laws of my country, and how to render justice." "Would to

God it were so," cried St. Felix. "I know not how to read, but I greatly fear that instead of justice there lie hidden under those bindings the science of avarice and the secret of how to foment quarrels and turn them to a judge's own profit. The law of Jesus Christ is the only safe book of law. If a man does not understand this he will never be able to understand any other; but if he does understand it, all others will be made as plain as day to him."

On another occasion, while St. Felix was conversing with the learned judge, the latter received the present of a calf from the plaintiff in an action, on the rights of which Biscia had to pronounce judgment. While St. Felix waited in the office the animal kept lowing. "Do you hear that seductive voice?" said he to the judge. "Just hearken how it keeps on crying out to you to give judgment in favour of the gentleman who sent you the gift. Take care, take care!" Ever after this little incident Biscia had the highest respect for the Capuchin lay-brother, sought him out and kissed his habit when he met him; nor was he ever known to refuse him an alms when solicited.

Many sought St. Felix's advice, and he never refused to give it; but if they did not exactly follow his directions, he was quick to rebuke them. There was a rich lady in Rome who was bowed down by a spiritual anguish for which she could find no relief, till she thought of appealing for counsel to the well-known begging-brother. When she had poured out her trouble of soul to him, he bade her sing some of his canticles and cast herself unreservedly on the divine pity, and by so doing she would, he was confident, be cured. Next time they met she told the Saint that she had done as he had bidden her, but still found no relief. Then he became angry with her, and declared that she was yielding to a diabolic temptation from which she had no desire to be released. But even while he rebuked her, he laid his hand on her head, and under his blessed touch her trouble of soul fled.

St. Felix never found himself at a loss, and even when he had to do with the Pope himself, was as ready of tongue as when he was conversing and singing with his favourite little children. Sixtus V—once Felix Peretti—was naturally drawn to his name-sake, the Capuchin brother, for he, too, had begun life as a poor shepherd-boy, and had subsequently been a Franciscan friar. When he grew to venerate St. Felix for his sanctity, it was not likely that he should forget these links which bound them together. The Sovereign Pontiff not only felt but testified to his deep veneration for the holy brother, for before he was raised to the See of Peter, he had had dealings with him which convinced him that he was a saint.

When Sixtus was Cardinal he headed a powerful party in the Sacred College bent on reform, and while many of its members hoped that he might one day be Supreme Head of the Church, others were equally inimical to him. He was well aware of this difference of opinion, which prevailed in the world as well as in the Sacred College, and one day he asked St. Felix what he thought would be the end.

"You only ask my opinion in jest," replied the Saint, "but your election to the Holy See will really take place. And when you are in the Chair of Peter, be careful how you govern the Church. If you are negligent, it would be better for you had you remained a simple friar."

No doubt these words of the Saint's remained in the mind of Cardinal Peretti. On his way to the Conclave which assembled after the death of Gregory XIII, he passed St. Felix going on his rounds. Stopping his coach, he called the brother up to him, and asked him of his charity to pray for him. "Eh?" said Felix, smiling, "so you want to be Pope, do you? Well, well, you shall have your wish. But be good, and do not forget the Franciscans."

In earlier days it had been Sixtus's custom to beg St. Felix to give him a loaf out of his wallet, which, out of devotion to the giver, he used to reserve to eat with his dinner; and when created Pope he manifested his devotion in the same way. One day when he was walking with his attendants near the church of the Trinità de' Monti, he espied St. Felix at a distance, and, sending for him, asked him to give him a bit of bread "for the love of God." The Saint dived into his wallet to seek for the best among his pieces, but the Pontiff told him to take no trouble, but to give him the first which came to hand. As it chanced, the piece which St. Felix drew out was a mouldy fragment of very coarse black bread.

However, in obedience to the Pope's request, he handed this to him with one of his ready remarks: "Excuse me, Holy Father," said he, "for you, too, are a friar."

There is no doubt that a great deal of St. Felix's personal influence, and the unwillingness shown to disregard his opinion, came from the wonderful power he possessed of reading the thoughts of men—a power in which the natural and supernatural met, merged, and worked together. He used this gift in a very manifold way, in matters so great as to involve the salvation of souls, and in others so small that the confusion of those whose secret weaknesses he revealed was all that was at stake.

There was a young lady who was undeniably worldly and still more undeniably silly. This girl, in a fit of foolish bravado, informed her friends that she meant to be a Capuchin nun, and excited a great deal of wonder and admiration by her statement. As she went downstairs after this little excitement she met St. Felix coming up. "Ah," said he in jest, laying his hand on her shoulder as he spoke, "did not your heart beat when you caught sight of me? I wonder it does not make you blush with shame to tell your friends that you mean to be a Capuchin nun, when you know you have not the slightest intention to become anything of the sort!"

That time he used his gift sportively, but at other times he made use of it to apply balm to hidden wounds. One day, after a lady had given him some bread as an alms, he looked at her long and fixedly, contrary to his usual custom. "What secret trouble is this which is breaking your heart?" he said at last. As the lady did not reply, he went on to describe exactly what it was that was making her miserable, though she had never breathed a word about her sufferings to any one. "But," he went on as he turned away, "it is nothing. Do not fear; say a rosary, and all will be well." And so it came to pass.

At times he was more severe with those whose secrets were made known to him. A fellow-countryman of his, Angelo of Cantalice, had, with native vengefulness, cherished a deep grudge against one of his neighbours, and finally resolved to do him an injury. In this spirit he, being in Rome, called on his fellow-townsman, and was surprised to find that St. Felix refused to speak to him. He insisted on knowing the reason of this slight. "Alas, Angelo," then said the Saint, "how can you yield to this diabolical temptation of revenge? Why, what evil has the man done you? If you go on indulging in this aversion, beware lest evil befall you and your family. Hasten to make friends with this man; otherwise you will be lost beyond remedy." So stupefied was Angelo that then and there he made known to the Saint his state of mind, and promised to follow his advice and reconcile himself without delay to the man he hated.

Marino, a Veronese gentleman, was entangled in an unlawful connection which he had several times tried to break, and had even sought the prayers of holy people to help him to do so; but again and again had he fallen back into his former life of sin. One day, as he was walking dejectedly in front of the Venetian Palace, he saw St. Felix approaching him hurriedly, and, before he could draw back, the Saint seized his two hands, and, shaking them roughly, said: "*Deo gratias.*" Marino, who had never in his life spoken to St. Felix, was much offended, and, casting off his hand, walked away. The holy brother, seeing that he was angry, said gently, "God be with you." The words, and the manner in which they were said, seemed to sink into Marino's soul; and all at once he saw his past life in a different aspect from what he had ever viewed it before. He detested the allurements from which he had found it impossible to detach himself, and thenceforward cut himself off completely from all occasions of sin.

It was not always necessary for the servant of God to be present in the body to read the thoughts of his friends even when, as in the following incident, nothing important was at stake. One Lent, while he was serving Mass, it was made known to him that one Paola, a great benefactress of the Capuchins, was crying her heart out from disappointment, because her husband had invited some guests to dinner, the preparation for which would prevent her from attending a sermon she wished very much to hear. No sooner was this state of affairs made known to St. Felix than he yearned to help his friend, and, calling another server to take his place, he went to Paola's house.

"But why do you fret about nothing?" were the words with which he greeted the weeping woman. "It is very good to hear the word of God, and it pleases Him that we should do so when we are able; but it pleases Him quite as much when we stay at home and do our work for Him there. Just now I was serving Mass, but, knowing of your trouble, I left that occupation which is so pleasing to God, in order to come and console you."

CHAPTER IX

SELF-ABASEMENT

IT MIGHT be almost said that St. Felix, moved by a secret divine impulse, went out of his way to take up the apparently anomalous position described in the last chapter. His duties as a begging-brother involved no apostolate, nevertheless, wherever sin had to be rebuked or trouble assuaged, he felt no shadow of doubt that it was his business to apply the remedy, and did so both promptly and efficaciously. Perhaps the most admirable part of his apostolate is the simplicity with which—docile to the interior guidance of the Holy Ghost—he undertook and accomplished work entirely foreign to his ostensible duties. Scarcely less admirable is the simplicity with which those around him accepted his self-appointed apostolate.

Some, moved by their devotion towards the holy brother, built castles in the air, and wondered whether his growing influence might not lead him, in spite of his want of learning, into the Sacred College. The veneration in which he was held by Sixtus V was no secret, and it occurred to some that the peasant-born Pontiff and austere ex-friar might testify to his devotion by the exaltation to the purple of the unlettered old Saint. They asked St. Felix, half jestingly, half tentatively, what he would do were the Pope to suggest such a thing. "What would I do?" he replied. "Why, I would beg His Holiness, if he really wished to do me honour, to hand me over to the public executioner to be whipped as a criminal."

There was little or no self-consciousness in St. Felix's composition, and he but rarely paused to consider the probable effect on others of his actions. Nevertheless, when tokens of respect and admiration were forced on him, his humility was deeply wounded. One of the Capuchin fathers, who had been the Saint's confessor for years, broke forth one day into exclamations of wonder at the favours lavished on him by God, and even called him the most blessed among men. "Ah, father," cried St. Felix, rebuking him with holy indignation, "call me rather the greatest reprobate among men!"

Sometimes God gave His servant special aids for the defence of his humility by revealing to him the thoughts of others and their intention to exalt him. One of the fathers in the convent had begged the gift of a few of his little crosses. He did not tell the Saint the purpose for which he wanted them, but, as a matter of fact, it was his intention to send them to a friend in Naples with a letter, which he had already written, in which he described the sanctity of the lay-brother and bade his friend treasure the crosses as indescribably precious, because made by him. The request for some of his crosses was far from unusual; nevertheless St. Felix, instead of giving them without comment, as he was wont to do, replied indignantly: "You ought to die of shame, you who say Mass every day, to tell such untruths. Why do you want to pass me, the most miserable of sinners, off as a saint? Your letter is full of falsities and falsehoods. Go, father, tear up at once what you have written. I will not give you a single cross till you have done so."

St. Felix disclaimed praise and rebuked flattery whenever they were offered to him, but we rarely find him going out of his way, as have done so many saints, to seek mortifications, whereby to draw on himself the contempt of those who might otherwise have admired him. His entire want of all fear of vain-glory was a most marked trait in St. Felix's character, and his lack of self-consciousness forbade the thought that he could be an object of admiration. He simply and honestly believed that his low birth and want of education, as well as his humble position of lay-brother and the undignified nature of his daily duties, would of themselves make him ridiculous in the eyes of men.

Needless to say that he was humble, for humility is the common note of the sanctity of the saints, and it is a truism to say that without humility there can be no sanctity. But humility in the saints takes different forms. There are some who might have been proud by nature, who yet, by hard fighting, won a profound humility. There are others who, seeing without experiencing the dangers of vain-glory, have lived in such dread of it as to spend their lives in seeking contempt, in order to ward off the peril. There have, again, been saints with such a spontaneously low opinion of themselves as to banish the very idea of vain-glory, and to the humility of this class that of St. Felix belonged to a pre-eminent degree.

It may be said without rashness that the danger of vain-glory did not exist for him. How else could he, during the closing months of his life, have been vouchsafed that divine revelation that he would, after his death, enter at once into glory? Had there been even a spark of vain-glory lying unelicited in his soul, such a revelation might have marred the Saint even at the eleventh hour.

He must have been aware of the high place he held in the world's estimation, and could not but have realised the strangeness and anomaly of a begging-brother of his antecedents being the adviser of those in high position, the admonisher of sinners, and the consoler of the dying. He knew all about it, for few men have been more gifted than he with shrewd observation and practical common-sense, yet he was not even moved by the sensation he caused. When all Rome—as will be related in another chapter—was astounded by his miracles, and the sick vied one with the other who could obtain the touch of his blessed, health-giving hand, he himself never found out that there was anything peculiar about him. Thus only can we explain the serene simplicity with which he walked through life.

If, however, St. Felix was too unconscious of self to seek out humiliations, none rejoiced more than he when insults came in his way; and the mortifications he loved most were not those purposely imposed by those who loved him, but those suffered at the hands of men who really despised him. Whatever happened he retained his serenity and patience.

One day, when he was returning home heavily laden, he came on a heap of timber lying across the street. His companion stepped over and walked on, but St. Felix, in trying to follow, lost his balance and fell, and not only strained his ankle, but cut his face with the bottles of wine broken in the fall. There he lay, quite helpless, with the wine and blood streaming down his face. Just then a rider came by, and the horse, frightened by the sight of the old brother struggling to regain his footing, shied violently and refused to pass the timber. St. Felix, seeing that he was the cause of the stoppage, cheerfully begged the rider's pardon for blocking the way; but the gentleman, looking contemptuously at him, spurred his horse over the obstacle and rode on.

Meanwhile, some bystanders had raised St. Felix from the ground and helped him home. As he limped along he protested against his awkwardness, and thus apostrophised himself: "Will you walk, ass, and not limp in this fashion! This accident serves you right, and I thank God for thus punishing your laziness." He had not given a thought to the rudeness of the horseman, but the latter could not so easily forget. The recollection of the old Capuchin lying maimed amid the broken glass, and his own indifference and insolence, filled him with remorse. He rode to the convent, and taking off his belt, hung it round his neck, and kneeling down, kissed the Saint's feet, and craved his forgiveness. Not only did he offer to pay all damages, but promised then and there to amend his life. St. Felix, full of confusion, also knelt down, and in his turn begged the gentleman's pardon for getting in his way. This incident was the beginning of a close friendship between the two, for the rider kept his promise, and completely changed his life.

St. Felix was occasionally subjected to humiliations far more galling to human nature than accidents such as the above, and met with genuine and contemptuous disapproval from those whose opinion he revered. One prelate in a high position was thoroughly displeased with the Saint's manner of winning souls, and gave directions that next time he called for alms at his palace he was to be brought before him. This having been done, the prelate abused him roundly for being a canting hypocrite, and commanded that he should be ignominiously turned out of the house and forbidden ever to beg there again.

This treatment rejoiced the Saint's humble soul, and on another occasion, when he was publicly humiliated in a still more painful manner, he rejoiced further. This time the reproaches came from one of his own Order, a Capuchin preacher of just renown for holiness and learning. He also objected to St. Felix's ways. One day he came upon the old brother in one of the squares, standing as was his wont, wallet on back, surrounded by children, singing hymns with them and other simple folk. The preacher lost his temper and upbraided the Saint severely. "How long are you going to abuse in this manner the patience of God and your superiors?" said he. "Hypocrite! When will you cease to cover your vanity under the cloak of simplicity? When will you have done with these follies whereby you seek to gain the reputation of sanctity? You only bring shame on your habit! What is the meaning of these ridiculous songs? You go your own way all day long. There is no such thing as rule or obedience for you; and yet you are so deluded that you do not see the scandal caused by your conduct."

The crowd stood in silent amazement at hearing their beloved old Brother Felix thus scolded; and wondered how he would receive the rebuke. They need not have suffered for him, for he did not seem to be in the least disturbed. "I will try, father, to profit by your words," he replied; "and to the end of my life I shall be grateful to you for speaking in this manner to me, and will try to prove my gratitude."

After such a scene it is pleasant to turn to those mortifications which were inflicted on him by the loving hands of friends. All, however, were the same to him, and he accepted every humiliation with genial simplicity, whether it came from friend or foe. Having been making his rounds one day, he was kept waiting for some time in a garden belonging to one of his benefactors, and occupied his leisure by gathering a bunch of flowers to take home to the sick friars in the infirmary. On the way home his companion, Brother Alessio, being seized by some spirit of mischief, took the opportunity of being in a quiet place to stick these flowers into St. Felix's hair and behind his ears, making him look like an old bacchante. When, however, he saw some people approaching, Alessio cried out: "Take them out— quick, quick! What will the people say if they see you like this!" "If you wish me to remove the flowers, why did you put them there?" quietly replied St. Felix. "Let the people say what they like. They can but mock me and take me for an old fool, which is just what I am."

On another occasion Cardinal Sforza being impelled, half by a spirit of teasing and half by a desire to test the brother's humility, stopped his coach, and, calling St. Felix up to him, stuck a flower behind his ear, and, placing an orange in his hand, bade him return to the convent, smelling the fruit the whole way. The Saint did as the Cardinal told him, and walked along quite regardless of the jeering remarks passed on him, till at the door of the convent, Brother Alessio, who was his companion, snatched away both flower and orange, saying: "Now, brother, you have suffered the mortification, and I will enjoy the fruit."

There is something in the two last incidents which forcibly recalls St. Philip's favourite ways of mortifying himself and his disciples; and the obvious conclusion to be drawn is, that his methods had passed into vogue, and that, in their manner of humiliating St. Felix, Cardinal Sforza and Brother Alessio were but imitating St. Philip's devices. It was, however, from that Saint himself that the holy Capuchin received and accepted a mortifi- cation of human respect which has come to be one of the best- known incidents of his life.

One day the two Saints—St. Philip with his usual group of disciples, and St. Felix, laden with his wallet and wine-gourds, and accompanied by Brother Alessio—met in the Via dei Banchi, near the old Mint; and as they stopped to speak together, all eyes were turned on them. The initiative in the fight for humiliations was taken by the Capuchin. "Are you thirsty?" said he to St. Philip; and on the latter replying in the affirmative, he continued: "Let me see, then, if you are a truly mortified man." Handing to him the large wine-gourd off his back, he bade him drink, which St. Philip did at once amid the jeers of the bystanders; though there were some among them who, gifted with more penetration, said: "Look, there is one saint giving drink to another."

"Now," said St. Philip in retaliation, after he had returned the wine-gourd; "I will see if you are a mortified man." So saying, he took off his hat, and, placing it on the other one's head, bade him go on with his business thus attired. St. Felix went off cheerfully, merely remarking that if any one stole the hat he would not be responsible for the loss. Thus he went on quite undisturbed, begging from house to house in his usual way, while the children, who were sure to be found wherever he was, ran excitedly after him, shrieking with laughter and hooting him. "Look, look," they cried, "look at Brother Felix with a hat on. Poor Brother Felix, have you got a headache?"

This went on till St. Philip, himself bareheaded, met him again near San Lorenzo in Damaso. With feigned anger he snatched the hat from St. Felix's head and rebuked him for the evil example of buffoonery which he was giving, adding that he intended to report his foolish behaviour to his superiors, who, he hoped, would impose a severe penance on him. Then both Saints went on their way rejoicing. Brother Alessio treasured the incident in his heart, and related it with its minutest circumstances at the process of his holy companion's beatification.

All readers of St. Philip's life know of his great affection for St. Felix, which seemed to be the outcome and expression of his devotion to St. Francis, whose faithful imitator he recognised in the holy lay-brother. It has been said by a biographer of St. Philip, that much as he loved St. Felix he would have loved him more had the Capuchin Saint possessed "lofty genius and wide culture." But we venture to think that it was because Felix was precisely what he was that St. Philip held him in such affection; for nowhere else could he have found one who, to such a pre-eminent degree, owed everything to God and nothing at all to nature. Rough, uncouth, unlettered, and uncultured, it required a St. Philip to gauge the wealth of heavenly wisdom possessed by the holy lay-brother. St. Philip knew and conversed with many

saints, yet we may believe that, when he pointed St. Felix out as
the greatest saint of whom the Catholic Church could then boast,
he was using no exaggerated figure of speech.

St. Philip owed his acquaintance with St. Felix to Persiano
Rosa, who took the begging-brother to visit him at San Girolamo.
Once introduced, he was a frequent visitor, and the benefit
received was mutual, for as St. Philip grew to know Felix and
drew forth his latent wisdom, he opened his own heart to him
and sought his advice.

His belief in the wisdom of the humble Saint is illustrated by
the manner in which he utilised it on behalf of St. Charles
Borromeo. That great Saint was occupied in compiling the rule
for his Congregation of Oblates—a subject which required much
thought. So intricate a matter did he hold it to be, that he would
not consider it completed until he had brought the document to
Rome, and laid it before St. Philip for his advice. Either from deep
humility or with the intention of making God's ways manifest,
St. Philip pleaded incompetence for such a task. But St. Charles
knew his friend's powers too well to accept a refusal, and
persuaded him to drive with him in his carriage, hoping to be
able at his leisure to overcome the Saint's resistance, and entrap
him into giving an opinion which he refused to give deliberately.
St. Philip accepted the invitation on the sole condition that he
should be taken wherever he desired. Accordingly, the coachman
was directed to drive to the Capuchin convent, and, when there,
and the two Saints having alighted, St. Felix was summoned to
speak with them.

Probably St. Charles knew nothing personally of the lay-
brother, though doubtless he had heard of his sanctity. That he
was ignorant and uncultured was self-evident, and it was with
amazement and not altogether with satisfaction that the Saint
of Milan heard St. Philip explain to this man the scheme of
the proposed Congregation, and follow up the explanation by
handing over the book of the rule to him, with the charge to
study it and make whatever changes and suggestions struck him
as advisable.

If St. Charles was annoyed the poor lay-brother was simply overwhelmed by the commission with which he was charged, and protested against it on the plea that he was not able even to read, and had no experience whatever on such a subject. But St. Philip knew what he was about, and insisted on handing over the manuscript to St. Felix, so that, having had it read to him, he might make whatever suggestions he thought fit.

Any one knowing St. Philip's ways might have thought that he acted thus for the sole purpose of mortifying the Cardinal Archbishop of Milan and the Capuchin lay-brother, each in his different way; but the event proved that his purpose was different. He knew St. Felix's inspired, yet simple and practical wisdom, and foresaw the value of his judgment on such a subject as the founding and ruling a Congregation. He was right, for when the brother returned the rule it was with two suggestions which delighted St. Charles by their pertinency.

St. Felix venerated all priests, but none so much as St. Philip, and if he could but obtain his blessing he was content. However far away he saw his familiar figure he would hasten to him and kneel before him, and then St. Philip would turn to him and embrace him. Twice are we told of meetings, when the Capuchin knelt before him and St. Philip silently embraced him, while a white light glowed on the countenances of the two Saints, who, after remaining motionless awhile, parted without exchanging a word. Sometimes, when St. Felix visited him at the Oratory, an impulse of veneration made St. Philip kneel at the lay-brother's feet for his blessing. Then a holy contest would ensue, for the Capuchin would throw himself also on his knees, and neither Saint would yield the point of humility to the other.

Rome is hallowed ground—hallowed by the blood of martyrs and the footsteps of many saints, but rarely do her ancient streets seem more holy than when we think of the constant meetings between St. Philip and St. Felix. The work of the latter took him up and down them all day long, while there is scarcely a spot that is not connected with the apostolate of the former. Thus—for Rome was not a large city—scarcely a day can have passed without their catching at least a glimpse of each other. Both

thirsted for suffering, and we read that the greeting they inter-
changed as they passed by was a reciprocal wish for an increase
of that which each desired. "May you have more suffering," said
they, for neither could think of a better salutation.

It was St. Philip's way to wish for the portraits of those
whom he revered. All readers of his life know of his picture of
Savonarola, and in his chapel at the Vallicella there hangs a
picture of St. Antoninus painted for him. In the case of St. Felix
he extended this mark of veneration to the living, and begged
Arpino, a painter of the day, to take his portrait for him. The task
was far from easy, for had Arpino ventured to ask the holy
Capuchin to sit to him, he would have refused his consent, even
at the risk of displeasing St. Philip. However, the painter obtained
a sitting surreptitiously, and sent the portrait when executed to
St. Philip, with a letter written on the back which explained how
he had contrived to execute the commission. The letter runs thus:
"Brother Felix came and I made him sit down and wait while they
fetched the bread and alms. I pretended to be doing something
else, and talked on to get a good look at him, and managed to
draw him without his knowing it. I send him to your reverence,
who will please bless me." This drawing, which St. Philip valued
highly during his lifetime, still exists, with the letter written on
its back.

Chapter X

The Famine

T. FELIX'S influence among his fellow-citizens had been steadily on the increase ever since he first began the habit of gathering crowds round him to sing the praises of God; but during the last seven years of his life it assumed proportions undreamt of before. To this latter portion of his life belong most of the numerous miracles, on account of which the name of thaumaturgus may well be given to him. Most canonised saints worked miracles; but St. Felix belongs to the class of those who, possessing the gift, are moved by the Holy Spirit to exercise it on all occasions and at all times, with a lavishness which introduces what must be called a vein of sportiveness into their wonder-working.

In 1580, a terrible famine devastated Rome; and a plague, consequent on it, filled the hospitals to overflowing. The impossibility of contending with the misery and starvation well-nigh drove the authorities to desperation. All classes were affected by the scarcity, and St. Felix had hard work to collect sufficient food for his Community and the large number of people who depended on it for sustenance. His tender heart bled for the destitution of the poor, and he would have liked to bestow on them all the alms he collected for the convent; and it was only when he was allowed to give them a few pieces from his wallet that he felt any peace of mind.

But occasions for such happiness as was afforded him by this scanty almsgiving were rare; for the superiors of the Capuchins did not share their holy brother's thirst for destitution. Charitable as they were on ordinary occasions, their anxiety for the

77

future of the Community under the present alarming circumstances partook almost of the nature of a panic. Far from
allowing St. Felix to give freely of their substance to the poor,
their sense of responsibility towards those under their charge
made them bid him be careful even of superfluities, and try to
obtain from benefactors more than enough for present needs, so
as to enable them to lay by something in case the scarcity should
increase. The Saint obeyed, but rarely had he found obedience
so hard.

Just at this juncture, when the Capuchin superiors were in
such thrifty dispositions, the authorities—or the directors of the
poor, as the annals of the time call them—expressed the desire to
utilise St. Felix's well-known influence among all classes, and lay
upon him the charge to collect alms throughout the city, not for
his own convent alone, but for all the poor, starving, and sick
citizens. At first the Capuchins would not hear of such a thing,
but being pressed on one side by the directors, and on the other
by St. Felix himself, they yielded, trusting tremblingly in
Providence.

No sooner had the Saint obtained the requisite permission,
than he set about his new work with the greatest alacrity. He first
surveyed the whole city, and in a few days had visited every
street, slum, and infected by-way, and made a note in his
retentive memory of the worst districts and poorest haunts. He
then set himself to supply the needs of the sufferers, and boldly
made his way into the houses of all those who were in a position
to give anything. His influence was marvellous, and all whom he
asked opened their hearts and purses. Thus he speedily collected
tons of food, clothing, and medicines.

When St. Felix undertook this work he pledged himself to
his superiors that his own convent and those immediately
depending on it should be his first care, and to this pledge he
faithfully adhered. But, however anxious he might be to provide
necessaries for the friars, he was most mindful of holy poverty,
which he considered to be more than ever binding on religious
in a time of common want. He had, in fact, a terror lest panic
about the failure of necessaries should degenerate into a desire

for superfluities. For the sick, however, he put all such fears aside. He never failed to visit the convent infirmary on his return from his weary rounds, and took its inmates anything that they wanted, even down to such little luxuries as the flowers which we found him gathering for them, when Brother Alessio utilised them to make his holy companion ridiculous.

All doors flew open at his bidding, and even those who might have refused their alms to others yielded to his persuasions. He reminded the rich that articles which they might cast away as useless were absolute necessaries to the starving poor, and that even gifts of this kind, given at little cost to themselves, would be repaid; and worn-out rags given to the suffering for love of God would be returned to them in another world under the form of gorgeous apparel. He would use the uncultured realistic eloquence with which he was gifted to move the hearts of men, and, walking unbidden into the splendid apartment of a palace, would tell the assembled guests that he had met our Lord half naked in the street, and hearing sounds of mirth inside the house, had come in to ask for something wherewith to cover Him, lest He should die of shame and cold. At the Saint's words the smart ladies and gentlemen would fly to their wardrobes and lay the contents at his feet. When he had thus made his way into the Spanish Ambassador's presence, and described with heartrending realism the misery he had witnessed, the Ambassador bade the Saint regard him thenceforward as his banker, on whom he might draw for anything he wanted.

Some very few refused to give, and usually these received their punishment then and there. St. Felix begged for some wine of a woman whose store was running low. She replied that she had but one cask left, which she required for her own use. The Saint passed on elsewhere; but when the woman went to draw her wine she found that the whole caskful had turned undrinkably sour.

Another time he was assisted in his fight against human selfishness by means which common report pronounced to be supernatural. He met with a rude refusal from a publican of whom he asked some wine. As he was turning away, a young man, unknown to all present, who appeared no one knew how, threw a gold piece on the counter, and bade the wine-seller supply St. Felix with all he needed.

More often the refusals with which the Saint met came, not from stinginess or churlishness, but from inability to give, and it was in cases such as these that he exercised his gift of working miracles with such profusion.

Princess Virginia Savelli was one of the most constant benefactresses of the Capuchins. To her the Saint one day applied for a certain medicine for the sick in the hospital. She told him with regret that she had none left, but sat down at once to her table to write an order for the drug, for him to take to the apothecary: "Why should you trouble to write?" said the Saint. "Tell Nanni, your steward, to come with me to the man. That will suffice without an order." "Alas, poor Nanni," the princess replied, "would that he were in a fit state to accompany you. Do you not know that every one of my servants is ill with this fever, and Nanni is worse than any?" "Perhaps it is nothing," said St. Felix. "Let us go and visit him together."

So the princess and the old Capuchin went, and found the steward in bed, in a state of great suffering and burning with fever. "Nanni, Nanni," said the Saint reproachfully. "What are you doing in bed? Get up at once, for I want you to help me." "Do not mock me, brother," moaned the poor man. "Cannot you see for yourself how ill I am?" "It is nothing whatever but laziness," retorted St. Felix. "Get up at once when I tell you, you man of little faith. You should not think twice when I tell you that you are wanted to do some work for God." Hearing these words Nanni got up, dressed himself, and went out with the holy brother, as if he had never been ill.

It was especially on behalf of the benefactors of his Order that St. Felix exercised his supernatural gifts. It was, in fact, his favourite way of proving his gratitude, a virtue the practice of which towards God and man was a marked feature in his character. Lavinia Carpi, one such benefactress, was rewarded more than once by miracles wrought on her behalf. In the course of his work of collecting for the famine-stricken poor, he called at her house to ask for a flask of wine. "Oh, brother," she cried, sorely distressed at not being able to oblige him, "what shall I do? Only yesterday we emptied a cask, and there are not even the dregs left; and I have no man in the house to broach another." "I dare say there is enough left for my purpose," he replied; "let us go and see." When, however, he turned the spigot, he found, as she had told him, only a few drops. Then he knelt down and, having prayed for a few moments, again turned the tap, and wine poured out with such force that it was evident to those present that the cask was quite full. So full indeed was it that its contents lasted the family three months, Lavinia was so overcome that she burst into tears, and declared that giving alms to Brother Felix was like putting money out at usury.

Another miracle akin to the last was worked by the Saint in favour of Lavinia. This time he called to ask her for some oil for his own Community, and in reply she told him that the vessel in which she kept it was empty and even washed out, but that if he would return the following day he should have as much as he desired. "It is all very well to put me off till to-morrow," exclaimed St. Felix; "but what are my poor friars to do to-day? They are fasting, and I have not even enough oil to cook them a dish of beans. You know perfectly well that you have what I ask for in the house, and are making excuses so that I shall not have it. Go and look, if you please, and you will find more than enough for me."

Lavinia's feelings were hurt by the Saint's incredulity and the false accusation of stinginess. Nearly weeping, she reminded him of her unfailing affection for the Capuchins, and challenged him to cite one instance when she had refused to give them anything she had. But as St. Felix, regardless of her expostulations, still insisted on her going to examine her oil-jar, she did so, and found it brimful. "Oh, Brother Felix," she cried as loud as she could, "what a miracle!" Hearing these words he joined her. "A miracle?" said he. "Pardon me, signora, but it was only your stupidity which caused you to make a mistake. None the less, thank God for His favours." Then, filling his flask, he shouldered his wallet and walked off.

Yet once more was good Lavinia Carpi the object of a visible supernatural favour. During the famine she had, either from carelessness or ignorance, neither winnowed nor dried her stock of wheat, which, by lying with its straw, turned mouldy. This—especially during the season of scarcity—was a great loss to her. When St. Felix heard of her misfortune he felt very sorry, and went into the yard where the corn was stacked, to see the extent of the mischief. Then, with the help of his companion he turned it over with a pitchfork, praying the while. Finally, after blessing the corn with the sign of the cross, he called Lavinia, and said: "The grain is quite sound now. Thresh it and grind it, and share it with Christ's poor."

Lavinia, full of gratitude, did as he bade her. Not only was the bread made from the meal sweet and good, but, to her amazement, she found that her store did not diminish. Seeing this manifest token of something more than natural, the idea came into her head to make cakes of the miraculous flour, to be given as medicine to the sick. A number were thereby cured, notably one Rutilio Benzoni, who was at death's door and had received the last sacraments. As soon as he had been persuaded to swallow a mouthful of Lavinia's cake his fever left him.

Cynthia Jacovacci was another constant benefactress of the Capuchins. She also was asked for some wine for the sick, and, like Lavinia, had just emptied the only available cask. Felix was very nearly as much at home in the house as she was herself, and his sole response to her refusal was to open the door and call the servant-maid. "Come, Mea," said he, "go to the cellar and see whether you cannot find me enough wine to fill my flask." "Indeed, brother," the girl replied, "it will be of no use, for this morning I tipped the cask up as far as I could, and nothing but thick sediment came out. I will go and look, but only to please you."

But in a minute or two Mea rushed back with the flask in her hand full of wine. "A miracle, signora," she cried to her mistress. "Just see the miracle Brother Felix has worked." "What are you chattering about, you simpleton?" said the Saint. "You told me there was no wine only to save yourself the trouble of drawing it. Let us thank God, and, as for you, try to keep a quiet tongue in your head." Cynthia, having gone to the cellar and seen with her own eyes that the cask was full, gave strict orders that Brother Felix should never be refused anything for which he saw fit to ask. As for him, he returned joyously to the convent, giving thanks to God the whole way home.

It would be impossible, and might be wearisome, to relate even a tithe of the miracles of this kind wrought by St. Felix as he went about, exercising the power given him by God over the humble creatures of food which it was the business of his life to collect. Some, however, of these miracles have an interest exterior to the supernatural element, and contain graphic touches of real life which reveal the kind of footing on which the Saint was with his benefactors, of the reverence in which he was held by them, and of his intimate knowledge of them and their concerns. On this account, at the risk of monotony and repetition, place must be found for them in a biography of St. Felix.

In one instance we find Vincenzio Carpoccio really affronted because the Saint refused to take his word when he said he had not wherewithal to satisfy his demands, and Erminia, the maid, was summoned to corroborate her master's statement. When she appeared, St. Felix, having made the sign of the cross on her forehead, twisted her round, and, laying his hand on her shoulder, pushed her before him all the way to the cellar, where the oft-repeated miracle was renewed. Carpoccio, being a practical man, did not wait to expatiate over the marvel as Lavinia or Cynthia might have done, but walked off with Erminia to the notary to testify on oath to what they had seen.

Again we find Paola Pusterla ordering her servant to fetch the wine asked for by St. Felix. The man, though quite aware that the cask was empty, did not dare say so for fear of his mistress's anger if he hesitated to accede to the Saint's request on however reasonable a plea. Turning the spigot for appearance's sake, he was amazed when a copious stream resulted from his action. Having confessed his deception to Paola, she ordered that the wine thus obtained should be treasured and given only to the sick, on whom it effected many cures.

Claudia de Fano—to mention one more incident of the same kind—was most devout to the holy son of St. Francis, and received a reward of her charity similar to those already related. The maid who had been sent to draw the wine rushed all over the house shrieking out that a miracle had been wrought. "Tell that idiot to stop screaming," said the Saint to Claudia. "There is no miracle at all, and if only the girl had gone at once when I bade her, and had not stood arguing, I should have been half way home by this time." Before he left the house, however, he swore Claudia to secrecy as to what had occurred, under penalty of never again seeing him under her roof. But the precaution was useless, for her cousin Gabriel was in the house, and had already become acquainted with the wonderful event. So great was the devotion towards St. Felix which it stirred up in him, that there and then he gave up everything to become a Capuchin lay-brother, though he was in every way qualified to enter the sacerdotal state.

CHAPTER XI

DOMINION OVER NATURE

HERE is one miracle which St. Felix wrought, out of mere kindness of heart, to relieve distress, which, though it does not belong strictly to the time of the famine, may well find a place among the other marvellous episodes connected with this period of his life. The occasion was slight, but the narrative is so rich in detail, and is so strongly illustrative of what must be called the sportive side in his exercise of supernatural gifts, that it possesses a special interest.

Maddalena de' Fannucci and her husband were dependent for a living on the rearing of silkworms, for the cultivation of which they had fitted up a room. One summer, a long continuance of wet weather had injured all the crops and natural products round Rome, and had wrought havoc with the mulberry-trees, on the leaves of which the silkworms were fed. One day, when St. Felix called at the house to beg some wine, Maddalena met him in tears, and was in a state of such evident trouble of mind that the Saint forgot all about his own errand, and anxiously asked the cause of her distress.

"Who could fail to be troubled?" she sobbed. "All my silkworms are sickening and cannot fail to die. I cannot find any dry leaves for them, and, as you may know, soaked and sodden leaves are like poison to them. All the care I have bestowed on them will be lost, and we shall be ruined."

"Never mind," replied the Saint; "do you go and fill my gourd, and I will see what I can do."

Maddalena, hoping for some supernatural aid, dried her eyes and hastened to fetch the wine. Meanwhile St. Felix went out and gathered a large armful of soaked leaves which he carried to the silk-room and threw all over the insects, nearly drowning them in the process. While he was thus occupied, Maddalena came in, and screamed out: "Stop, brother, stop, before you have killed them all!" But he continued to strew the leaves and sprinkle the silkworms, invoking St. Francis aloud as he did so. Then, without a word, he took the wine and left the house.

The poor woman continued to rail equally against fate and the holy Capuchin. "Oh, cruel, cruel brother," she moaned, "you have indeed ruined me. What possessed you to serve me thus in return for my alms? I could pity your ignorance, but that, alas, will not save my silkworms." When her husband came home late in the evening she told him what had occurred, and they agreed that the only thing to do was to shut the door of the insects' room, to prevent the house from being infected by the smell of their carcases. This done, the couple went to bed, trying to make the best of their misfortune, and prepared to make a clearance next morning of the dead insects.

The husband cherished a ray of hope which he vainly tried to impart to his wife. Felix being a saint, he argued, would never have acted so madly without reason; and his invocation of St. Francis, his silent departure, and the absence on his part of all contrition for his mistake, looked at together, made the good man suspect that there might be more in the occurrence than met the eye. But Maddalena's common sense made her put more trust in the deadly properties of the wet mulberry leaves than in the possibility of a miracle.

The husband was right. When Maddalena got up in the morning and put her feet in her slippers, she found them full of cocoons which the silkworms were hard at work spinning. She rushed to the insects' room, where she found the same energetic work going on, more cocoons having been spun in a single night than were usually produced by the little creatures in a fortnight. The news of the marvel soon spread throughout Rome; and when the silk—the result of that wondrous spinning—was woven, people came in numbers to ask for fragments to keep as relics.

As we read narrative after narrative of the way St. Felix exercised his miraculous gifts, it is impossible not to ask ourselves why it was that he was moved to use his supernatural power with such prodigality, and often, as it seemed, on such trivial occasions. In the many miracles which are recorded of the multiplication of food in the hands of the Saint, it must have been the simplicity of his intercourse with heaven, combined with a practical and business-like sense of economy, which, at a time when he was straining every nerve to procure a sufficiency of provisions, made him prefer to seek the direct intervention of God rather than waste the charity of those who were willing to give. The same thriftiness made him work a miracle rather than lose some wine procured under difficulties.

From stress of poverty the Saint usually collected wine in gourds, the Community not being able to afford him such large flasks as were habitually used. One day, during the famine, when he and Brother Illuminato were returning home after a long, weary day's work, the Saint, in removing his load from his back, hit one of the wine-gourds against the wall and split it in half. Illuminato, who was probably irritable with fatigue, turned angrily on his companion. "See what you have done," he cried. "There is the result of a day's labour lost! God forgive you your clumsiness, Brother Felix. At least try to save what few drops are left." "Calm yourself, brother," replied the Saint, "and leave it to God to remedy the disaster." Then, making the sign of the cross over the broken gourd, he placed it in Brother Illuminato's hands, not only entire but full of wine. "There, brother," he said with his usual gaiety, "are you happier now? In future do not put yourself out about anything that does not offend God."

Whether in working miracles or in the more ordinary events of life, we always find St. Felix the same. Nothing seemed to cloud his brightness or upset his patience. During the famine a necessitous priest, seeing the amount of goods which the Saint received for the mere asking, conceived the astute idea of turning this success to his own advantage. Setting forth very early one morning, so as to obtain a start of the Capuchin mendicants, he visited the houses of the more generous among their benefactors, and informed them that Felix, being ill, had commissioned him to collect alms in his stead. The impostor met with success even beyond his expectations, though, unfortunately for him, it could not but be short-lived; for as soon as the Saint appeared on the scene the deception was discovered. Those who had been duped were furious, and wished to take prompt measures for the severe punishment of the impostor; but the Saint interceded for him, pointing out that he himself was the one to suffer most, as he had lost the offerings of his benefactors, and that if he forgave the injury others might well do so also. "Let us see Christ in this priest," said he, "and let us provide for him so that he may not again be thus tempted to sin." Privately, however, he rebuked the priest for the fraud, which was particularly abhorrent to him on account of his high veneration for the sacerdotal state. Having extracted a promise from the offender never again to resort to dishonest means of livelihood, the Saint undertook to provide from his alms for his future necessities.

During the plague, or epidemic, which accompanied the famine, St. Felix worked many other miracles besides those of the multiplication of food. As a rule, during that time of scarcity and sickness, whenever he exercised the tremendous power of healing given him by God, he took as his instrument one of those simple articles of food which he spent his days in handling. His devotion to the sick was great, and to them he gave whatever time he could spare from his begging. He dedicated to them the greater part of his Sundays, which he spent in the public hospitals, tending the patients, ministering to their wants, and—needless to say—looking after their souls. Here, as outside in Rome, his panacea for all suffering, mental and physical, was sacred song. If he found any in fear of death, or troubled by anxiety about their temporal affairs, or subjected to any other temptation, he used to sing to them some of his rough canticles; and the words, or, still more, the Saint's manner of singing, brought peace to the soul and, more than once, health to the body. But to effect this last he usually had recourse to more direct means.

While visiting in the Hospital of the Lateran, he found a man lying at the point of death. The only question he asked of the attendants was whether they had given him any wine. Not only did they reply in the negative, but they added that the doctor had expressly forbidden its being given. "Nevertheless," said the Saint, "it would be well that he had some." With these words he himself poured out some wine and forced a few drops down the throat of the dying man, who from that moment began to recover.

Another day he visited a man lying in the Hospital of Santo Spirito, who was so near his end that the attendants, not to lose time, had brought a bier to the bedside, and were waiting only for the breath to have left the dying man's body to carry him off for burial—a proceeding which both the patient and his nurses seemed to regard as very usual.

"What are you about there, burying a living man?" asked the Saint, standing over the bed. The attendants replied that though it was true the man was alive he would in a few minutes cease to be so, and that it was needless waste of time for them to leave him. But St. Felix insisted that they were talking nonsense and that the man would not die.

"You are no doubt a very holy old friar," replied one of the others good-humouredly, "but you know nothing about this sort of thing. You leave this business to us. I tell you that he is to all intents and purposes as dead as if he had been a week in his grave."

Without arguing further the Saint went to fetch some wine from the sacristy of the hospital chapel, and poured a few drops down the dying man's throat. To the astonishment of those present he opened his eyes, sat up, and from that moment gradually recovered.

As the sanctity of the holy Capuchin became better known, he was frequently sent for to attend the sick-beds of the more considerable personages in the city, not to cure them, but to console them, and, if necessary, help them to die well. Often, however, the result of his visit was to restore health to the body as well as to the soul.

Orsina, Duchess of Aquasparta, was in great danger from haemorrhage. She could swallow no food and her strength was rapidly declining. In her extremity she sent for Brother Felix to console her. Into her bed-chamber he walked, summoned hastily in from the hot street; and, as soon as he reached her side he dived into his wallet, and, drawing out a piece of bread, handed it to her. "Eat this," said he, "and you will live;" and she, having obeyed the strange direction, recovered.

Santi Marrazino was seriously ill with but little chance of recovery. He too sent for St. Felix. "Eh, Santi," was the latter's greeting; "whatever is the matter with you? You look as exhausted as if you had been doing a hard day's work." "I am preparing for death," replied the sick man. "Gently, gently, not so fast," interrupted the Saint gaily. "There is plenty of time yet." Then, taking a quince from his bag, he bade Marrazino smell it; and, as he did so, all dangerous symptoms disappeared.

Paolo Zeffiro was dying. So near death was he supposed to be that, in the words of the narrative, "the doctors went no more near him, and the priests never left him." When matters came to this pass his wife Ortensia sent for Brother Felix to help Paolo to die well, and to console herself. The Saint came with all speed when he was summoned, and, looking steadily at the sick man as he lay, apparently expiring, on his bed, said: "Your husband will not die." "But," pleaded Ortensia, "I regard him as one dead now." "Never mind what you think," replied St. Felix; "it will be just as I tell you. Take this cake I have brought with me. Give him half of it to eat, and he will soon be well."

Ortensia could not help smiling in the midst of her grief, for it was days since Paolo had been able to swallow anything, and there was something ludicrous in the idea of his being able to eat the coarse bread produced by St. Felix. However, to satisfy the old Brother, for whom she and her husband had a deep affection, she placed a crumb of the cake on the dying man's lips. He sighed, opened his eyes, and, taking the remainder of the bread in his hand, ate it of his own accord, and rapidly returned to life.

CHAPTER XII

THE HEALING HAND

As YEARS went on the gift of healing became so much a part of St. Felix's intercourse with men that it seemed to flow spontaneously from his blessed hand as he walked through life. It is, however, our purpose to relate only a few of such miracles, for there would be but little interest in an enumeration of cures, with a string of names which throw but little light on the Saint's own individuality.

It has already been shown how much St. Felix loved children, and how they on their side regarded the child-like Saint as their special property. The account of a great miracle wrought by him on a child in 1578, which has been handed down in minute detail, is full of that beauty and charm which are the invariable accompaniment of every incident of his life which is connected with children.

A little boy named Fulvio Fosco, the child of well-to-do parents, had lost the sight of both eyes in consequence of an attack of small-pox. The boy, who was only six years old, felt his infirmity acutely, and fretted and cried without ceasing, and no affection or amusement could comfort him. He had, presumably, heard St. Felix's miracles spoken of, and he became possessed by the idea that if only the Capuchin Brother could be fetched and induced to make the sign of the cross over his eyes, he would see. This idea now became the subject of renewed fretfulness, and his mother and nurse, accustomed to his constant moans, petted and soothed him, but paid no more attention to this particular desire than they would had he fretted to have the moon given to him.

So persistent, however, was he that at length, for very weariness, his parents thought it better to send to ask St. Felix to come. They were not among the Capuchins' benefactors, and the holy brother was not known personally to any one in the house. As soon as Fulvio heard that his request had been so far granted, his impatience for the Saint's arrival was painful to witness, and to satisfy him a maid was posted at a window to watch for and announce the first appearance of the Capuchin Brother.

When the Saint's approach was reported by the maid, Fulvio cried out, "Quick, quick, let me go to meet him. Do not let him come up our wretched staircase lest he should trip up and hurt himself." Catching the infection of the child's trembling excitement, the maid snatched him up in her arms and carried him downstairs, followed by his parents.

As soon as St. Felix was admitted to the house, Fulvio, groping about till he felt the friar's habit, threw himself at his feet and clung to them. "Oh, dear Brother Felix," he said, sobbing, "I am quite, quite blind. I cannot see even the light of day. Do help me." The Saint was deeply moved by the child's tears, and said: "But, my son, what do you want me to do?" "Oh, dear brother," sobbed Fulvio, "I beg you for the love of God to make the sign of the cross over my eyes, and then I shall see."

"My son," replied St. Felix gravely, "as for me, I am the worst of sinners. But have you sufficient faith in the holy sign of our redemption to believe that it will restore your sight?" "Oh yes," cried the boy, "I have faith; I do believe. Make haste and sign me with your blessed hand, and I shall see."

"Well," said the Saint after a moment's thought, "let us all kneel down and say five *Paters* and *Aves* very devoutly." He led the prayers, but could hardly proceed, so moved was he by the sight of the little child kneeling with his hands and sightless eyes raised to heaven, sobbing out the holy words convulsively. The prayers finished, St. Felix rose silently to his feet, made the sign of the cross over the boy's eyes, and at once left the house with his companion. Barely, however, had he crossed the threshold, ere he heard Fulvio's voice shouting joyfully: "Father! Mother! I see! Brother Felix has cured me." And then all who had been present cried out that it was the most wonderful miracle, and that the Capuchin Brother was indeed a saint.

Hearing these exclamations and, as was his wont, feeling annoyed at the praises of himself, St. Felix turned back and abruptly re-entered the house. "You simple creatures," said he to the members of the household, who all seemed nearly beside themselves; "what is all this nonsense which you are talking about Brother Felix? He is a miserable sinner and has had nothing to do with this child's cure. It is his faith alone which has wrought the miracle. So be quiet. Give glory to God, and do not say one word more about Brother Felix." He then turned away sharply as though annoyed; and, slamming the door behind him, returned to the convent.

Brother Matteo, the Saint's usual companion during his later years, experienced more than once the benefit of his gift of healing. One morning this brother awoke with violent inflammation in his eyes; and, when St. Felix went to fetch him to start on their round, he declared that it would not be possible for him to go out in such a state. "But," he added simply, "if you, Brother Felix, will make the sign of the cross over my eyes I shall be quite well." "Oh, you want something to gossip about, do you?" replied the Saint somewhat roughly. "But, well, well, kneel down and say five *Paters* and *Aves*, and we will see what will happen." Then, St. Felix having made the sign of the cross over him, Matteo pronounced himself cured and able to go out.

Once more was he healed in a similar way. During the preparations for a procession of the Blessed Sacrament a log of wood fell on his head and cut him severely. He went to the infirmarian, who, in his turn, sent him to St. Felix as one better able to help him. "What," said the Saint, "first your eyes and now your head? You certainly are resolved to have something to talk about. However, come to my cell and we will see what can be done."

The sign of the cross was the instrument habitually used by the Saint in his miracles of healing. He hoped to conceal himself behind the sacredness of the symbol, and fondly hoped that those whom he made whole would attribute their cure solely to the power of the cross, and would ignore him of whom God deigned to make use. Praise was abhorrent to the humble Saint, and dread of drawing it on himself might, but for his simplicity, have made him refrain from using his miraculous gifts. Sometimes the fight between humility and charity was severe, but over and over again the latter won the victory, with the result that few saints have existed more prodigal with their miraculous power than he.

But he always had a primary regard for the souls of those who sent for him. A young man named Marc Antonio Muti, who bore but an indifferent character, being dangerously ill, called in the Saint with the hope that he would cure him. But first St. Felix sat down by his bed and talked seriously to the youth and his mother. He considered that she had been largely responsible for her son's misdemeanours, and he stoutly refused to make the desired sign of the cross over the sick man until Muti had promised faithfully to amend his ways, and his mother had equally promised to help him to keep his resolutions.

At times, though he could never quite harden his heart against sinners, he could be very severe in the expression of his displeasure. Pietro Straccalini was in such agony of pain from ulceration in his leg that, having found no relief from ordinary remedies, he sent for a woman who had the reputation of being able to charm away diseases. After she had subjected him to her incantations, it pleased God to allow him to grow worse instead of better, so that his life was really endangered by the poisoned state of his blood. Just then Felix called at Pietro's house to beg for alms, and hearing from the servants all about their master's illness and the magical remedies applied, he walked into the sick man's room in a state of great indignation.

"What does all this mean?" he exclaimed, examining everything in the room. "Women, signs, oils, ointments, bandages, incantations, and all manner of devilry! Folly, folly!" Then, turning to the sick man, he asked him how he felt; and Pietro replied that he was dying. "Nonsense, not a bit of it," returned the Saint, and taking Pietro's legs in his two hands he beat them together with all his strength, invoking St. Francis as he did so. The man screamed with agony, but the more he screamed the more did the Saint persist in his severe treatment until, thinking he had punished the poor wretch sufficiently, he desisted and left him. As soon as Pietro had recovered from his rough handling he found that all symptoms of blood-poisoning had disappeared; and, when a few days after he was able to visit St. Felix, he promised him faithfully that he would never again have anything to do with magic.

Where the Saint's charity was most tried, and where he was sorely tempted to refuse the boon asked, was where flattering words were used as a means of persuasion. The Marchesa di Riano was taken ill, with violent pain, and she, with the prevailing impulse, sent for the old lay-brother to help her. "Brother Felix," said she, as soon as he entered her room, "seeing that God, on account of your singular perfection, has given you the power of relieving maladies which will not yield to human remedies, do have compassion on me, and deliver me from these torments by making the sign of the cross over me." At the sound of these words St. Felix turned and would have left the room; but human respect restrained him, for the sick Marchesa was a very grand personage. Nevertheless he spoke his mind and reproached her for thus indulging in flattery. "If," added he, "I received my deserts at the hand of God I should this moment be cast into hell, for I am a sink of all vices. But if you have faith in the holy cross of Christ, He may perchance—in spite of my sins—heal you by its virtue. But give glory to God alone, and confusion to Brother Felix."

A favourite way with the Saint of covering his wonderful gift was to throw ridicule on the doctors who were attending the sick to whose aid he was called in. Muzio Mattei was given over by his physicians, and was advised by them to receive the last sacraments. He then made his will and prepared himself for death, and sent for Brother Felix to help him, and talk about the things of God. "Most willingly will I go to him," cried the Saint when the message reached him. "Christian gratitude, if nothing else, would compel me to it, for he has been a good friend to us."

"Courage, Muzio," he said cheerfully as he entered the sick man's room. "So the doctors have given you up, have they? All I can say is, that they have not studied those old books of theirs to much profit. In spite of what they say you will live to make another will!" As he spoke he laid his hand on Muzio's burning brow. The man, who felt his fever abating under the blessed touch, seized the Saint's hand and kissed it; but St. Felix, doubtless feeling that virtue had gone out of him, snatched it away and left the room. "Oh praised be God," cried Muzio, "the hand of the doctor could not touch my malady, but the hand of Felix, without writing any prescription, has restored me to health. I have learnt that even for the complaints of the body it is better to call in the help of saints before we call in that of physicians. Under the treatment of the latter I was as one dead, whereas under the treatment of a saint I have been restored to life."

When, however, it was a question of peril, not to himself but to one dear to him, Muzio forgot the resolutions made on his own sickbed. His son Mario, a lad of fourteen, fell seriously ill, and his father sent for more than one of Rome's best physicians. The boy, however, grew worse instead of better, and was ere long pronounced to be in a state of considerable danger. Fortunately, when he was at his worst, St. Felix happened to call at the house for alms, and Muzio, remembering, though tardily, how he had been cured, sent for the brother to lay his hand on the boy, which he did with blessed effect.

The doctors often smiled at the Saint's contempt for their skill, which, however, did not decrease their admiration for him. Thus, when in their presence St. Felix cured one Bernardo of an internal abscess, they gladly acknowledged his superior power; and one of them remarked with a smile, that to be a really good doctor a man should be a saint.

One of the cures most pleasant to relate—on account of its subject—is that of Sister Felice, the Saint's faithful friend, to whose care he confided the terrible breastplate with which he chastised his body. She had for some years been afflicted with a tumour and had more than once asked him to cure it. Either from humility, or from a desire for her sanctification, the Saint had as often refused, but at last he yielded, and made over her the life-giving sign of the cross. "Do not forget," said he after curing her, "that I am only poor old Brother Felix who says a great deal but does nothing."

It may be remarked that in his cure of Muzio Mattei, as well as in that of his son, St. Felix effected his end by laying on his hand instead of by making the sign of the cross. As a rule, however, he was unwilling to employ this means, as it brought his own share in the miracle into greater prominence. On one occasion at least virtue flowed from his healing hand without his own volition. The Duchess Cesarini being in great pain with a quinsy, sent for the Saint and vainly implored him to lay his hand on her throat. Then she, full of faith, seized his hand and applied it to the place, obtaining thereby immediate relief.

Monsignor Andrea de' Grandi was suffering such tortures of pain in his head that he thought he should go out of his mind, and sent for St. Felix to lay his hand on his head. But the Saint was obstinate, saying that the ass of the Capuchin Community had no business to take such a liberty with one in this prelate's high position. In his despair De' Grandi bethought him of commanding the old Saint in the name of holy obedience to accede to his wishes, and St. Felix, yielding to him, cured him with his touch. This event impressed the prelate so deeply that in after life he sent for the humble Saint whenever he found himself in a dilemma, or wanted advice about the grave matters connected with his official position.

Sometimes, though rarely, St. Felix did not wait to be asked to work a cure, but volunteered it in an almost sportive manner. Attilio di Velletri was in torture with gout in his knee, and was in such fear of being touched that he cried out as soon as any one threatened to approach him. St. Felix walked into the room, and, in spite of Attilio's warning cries, went straight up to his bed, seized the affected leg roughly, and, having rubbed it violently, went away. Attilio, feeling himself to be cured, got up at once and walked to the convent to thank his benefactor.

One more miracle, which filled Rome with astonishment, must be related. One day, when he was alone—having despatched Brother Matteo on business in another direction—he passed the house of a woman with whom he was acquainted. Hearing piercing shrieks he ran in to see what was the matter, and found her with an infant, apparently dead and already wrapped in a shroud, lying in her arms. "Oh brother," she cried when she saw him, "I am in despair, for my days are numbered. Look at this babe whom you have so often fondled—here he lies dead, and I, his cruel mother, have killed him by my carelessness." When the Saint had succeeded in calming her she went on to tell him that, having the child in bed with her, she had lain on him in her sleep and smothered him. "And oh," she continued, "the worst is to come. Twice before have I done the same thing, and my husband has vowed that if it were ever to happen again he would kill me. Pray for me that my sins may be forgiven, for in a short time I shall be no more."

The Saint, full of compassion, went and stood over the body of the child where the woman had laid it before speaking to him. Then, taking it in his arms he pressed it lovingly to his heart and said to the mother: "You are a simpleton. Do you not see that your child is only asleep?" Giving the babe a gentle box on the ear he put it, now smiling, into her arms; and then ran away, closing the door behind him.

Very soon the news of the miracle was all over the neighbourhood, and, among others, Matteo heard of it before he rejoined the Saint, from whom, by dint of questioning, he extracted the truth. "Listen, Brother Matteo," said St. Felix, when he had narrated the incident, "if ever you come to hear anything of this sort about me, I command you not to talk about it so long as I live. This I command you in the name of our Lord Jesus Christ. If you disobey me you will have to render an account at the day of judgment."

CHAPTER XIII

THE GIFT OF PREDICTION

SOMETIMES, even while performing a miracle of healing, St. Felix would predict the future conditions of those to whom he was asked to minister; and this gift conduced to his reputation of sanctity more, perhaps, than the cure itself. There was one incident, connected with an accident to a child who fell from a window at some height from the ground, which at the time caused a great sensation. Some of the witnesses declared that the child was dead, and that St. Felix restored it to life; but, be that as it may, he predicted the little one's future with unerring certainty. He knew the child's parents, and, having, heard of the accident, hastened to their house, where he found a number of relatives and friends gathered round the unconscious infant. Seeing the Saint, the mother ran forward and, clasping his feet, implored him to restore her child to her. He stood over the little body, praying silently for some time, and then, turning to the woman, said: "Take comfort, the angels have saved your little one from death. Be sure that he will recover completely; but take care of him, for he will be a Capuchin." When the child reached man's estate, his Franciscan vocation verified the Saint's gift of prescience.

A lady of his acquaintance, a benefactress of the Order, named Lavinia de' Cavalieri, was in great danger in childbirth; and, as was usual in all emergencies, St. Felix was sent for to give her his blessing. "Have no fear," said he, turning to Lavinia's husband; "ere long a son will be born to you. Call him Francis." Later, when the mother was convalescent, he visited her, and found her with the infant—duly named after the seraphic Saint—

in her arms. He took him from her and fondled him as he was wont to do with babes. "Oh," said he, gazing intently at him, "what a lovely, winning child; but, Signora, take care not to grow too fond of him." Though she questioned him anxiously he would say no more, but his meaning was made clear to her when her little Francis was taken to heaven a week later.

Often, when called in to visit the sick, St. Felix, without laying his healing hand on them as requested, contented himself with predicting either their death or recovery. If he saw that the person would recover, he usually concealed his gift of prescience under a tirade against the ignorance of doctors. "Really," he exclaimed impatiently, when he found Camilla Zeffiri's house shut up because—so the porter told him—she was lying at death's door, and given over by her physicians. "Really, people believe in the truth of a doctor's words as if they were the Gospel!" Leaving word with the servant that they were all mistaken, and that his mistress would without fail recover, he went his way. The accomplishment of the Saint's prediction filled Camilla and her household with wonder and admiration.

Silvio, son of this lady, had lamed himself by an accident. The injury being pronounced incurable the boy fretted himself ill, and was supposed to be going into a decline. Camilla, in her misery, sent for St. Felix to console her. He smiled when she told him of the physician's verdict, and shook his head knowingly. "Really," said he, "the skill of these expert doctors is like an enigma to me; and they often give the wrong answer. Come, cheer up, and laugh at what your wise doctors say. Your Silvio will neither die of decline, nor will he be lame for life; so you see you have no cause for tears." The mother believed St. Felix's words; nor was she deceived.

Although, as can be seen from the instances cited, St. Felix frequently predicted the return to health of those whose life was despaired of, he as frequently foretold death in cases where no danger was suspected. The Cardinal of Pisa was lying sick; and Felix, who had been called in to visit him, pressed his hands and pronounced his favourite ejaculation, *Deo gratias*. "Return thanks to God, Monsignor," he continued. "Do so as fervently as you can, for you have great cause for thanksgiving. And do you, all of you, say *Deo gratias* for your master," he added, turning to the attendants.

The Cardinal had a very high opinion of the holy Capuchin's sanctity and illumination, and was delighted to hear his words. "Yes," he said, taking up the Saint's theme and addressing his attendants, "let us thank God, for behold here is a man filled with the Holy Spirit; and indeed, since he has been in the room, I begin to feel better." "You are mistaken," St. Felix went on to say. "It is not on account of your return to health that you have reason to thank God, but for another and far greater reason. Rejoice and give thanks, because your name is written in the book of life, and ere long God will call you to Himself." Not long after this the sick man's symptoms changed for the worse, and during his agony the Cardinal repeated the words *Deo gratias* over and over again, and died with every appearance of joy.

Among St. Felix's greatest friends were a stone-carver named Alessandro Poggi and his family, whose house he often blessed by his presence. Poggi's wife fell ill, and the Saint, seeing in the spirit that she would not recover, visited her each day and talked to her about death and eternity. So unwilling was she to accept death that her state made him very anxious. He took her daughter Girolama, a girl of sixteen, into his confidence, and, confiding to her that her mother must surely die, urged her to do her utmost to persuade her to prepare for death. But Girolama would not even listen to his words, and implored him for the love of our Lord to use his power with God to prolong her mother's life. "I am so young," said she; "pray that she may be left to me, at least till I am a little older."

"Daughter," replied St. Felix reproachfully, "you really should have more wisdom, and not give way to sorrow in this manner. Your mother will die, I tell you, and God will not reverse His decree. So if you really love her, remain by her side, and never leave her until you have moved her to contrition and confession of her sins. Try to induce her to receive the last sacraments, for the devil will do his utmost to disturb her. I will do what I can, but do you exert yourself, for there is no time to lose."

That very day the woman became worse; still, she could not be persuaded to prepare herself for death. St. Felix remained in the room, not near her bedside, but kneeling in a corner with his face covered; and thus he stayed for hours. When at last Girolama came to him and told him that all was over, he rose to his feet and stood over the body. Then he said: "Praise be to God who has overcome in the hard battle. And you, child, console yourself, for though you have no mother on earth you have one in heaven."

Mention has already been made of Princess Savelli as one of the greatest benefactresses possessed by the Capuchins. Well was it for those who opened their hearts and hands at the call of the holy son of St. Francis, for verily they had their reward on earth as well as, we may feel assured, in heaven. The Princess had fallen into a weak state of health, and, having tried every conceivable remedy, she became weary of her long medical treatment, and dismissed her doctors, declaring that death itself would be preferable to the worry and discomfort she suffered at their hands.

She was lying in bed, prostrate in spirit, when St. Felix came to visit her. He began to talk about her ailments, and made a retrospect of the course of her illness, describing every detail and enumerating the many systems and experiments tried on her by her medical advisers, till, in her astonishment, she asked him who had told him all the particulars which he had thus described. But he continued, without answering her question, "Be of good comfort, Signora, for your health will be restored to you, though not completely, for a certain remains of weakness will tend to your sanctification. Let me, moreover, tell you that it is God's will that this partial restoration of your health should be effected by natural means. So recall your physicians forthwith, and let them prescribe for you as their skill prompts them, and do you accept all that you have to endure at their hands as a penance for your sins. Thus will your soul be purified."

It was not only life and death, sickness and health, which called forth the exercise of the Saint's gift of reading the future. There were but few events in life which did not come under its dominion; indeed, the future conditions of all his friends seemed to lie mapped out before him. A young lady, Lina Fiambetti, in whom he was interested, was engaged to be married to one Gambara. But obstacles were put in the way of her marriage, and in her dilemma the girl appealed for help to the old lay-brother.

"Ah," said he with a sigh when he had listened to her story, "better far for you would it be to renounce marriage altogether, and consecrate yourself to God in a religious house." This idea was not at all to Lina's liking, and she replied that she was quite bent on matrimony. "Well, well, so be it then," replied the Saint. "All these difficulties in the way of your marriage with Gambara will be smoothed away, nevertheless you will not marry him. He whom you will marry will subject you to untold crosses and sufferings."

Still, however, Lina would not take warning, and all came to pass as St. Felix had foretold. When—all impediments being removed—she was on the eve of marrying Gambara, he was killed in a quarrel. Her heart had not been much in the alliance, and so disappointed was she at the grand wedding preparations being made for nothing that she almost immediately gave her hand to another suitor. This man proved to be a veritable tyrant, by means of whom she led a life of martyrdom which must have often made her think of the old Saint's advice.

Thus did St. Felix go through life doing good to all men, and showering on them benefits of all degrees, from restoration of life and health down to the removal of small and fleeting disappointments. Out of his abundance of divine gifts he gave freely, but we rarely come across cases of his receiving anything in return, though there were such exceptions. Intercourse with all his good benefactors must have been pleasant to him, but in two cases we find him leaning on his friends for help and sympathy. One of these was his faithful confidante Sister Felice; and about the other, Agatha Fanini, the Saint's biographers tell us that he found such solace in her company and holy conversation that it formed his chief consolation upon earth. So persistent, however, was his spirit of gratitude, that in no case would he receive benefits without repaying them in full measure;

and his treatment of Agatha was no exception. She was a married woman, and one day, having first exhorted her to accept God's visitation heroically, he told her that ere long her husband would be condemned to the galleys for assaulting a lawyer. This came to pass, but so energetically and effectually did St. Felix use his influence that the man was pardoned.

All this time, while he was astounding Rome by his miraculous gifts and doing the work of an apostle, while he was restoring the sick to health, preparing souls for death, drawing all men to him for aid and consolation, and acting as a beneficent spirit to all whom he knew, the routine of his life, as we have tried to describe it in preceding chapters, remained unchanged. His days of toil about the streets and his nights spent in prayer succeeded each other with the same unbroken and holy monotony; and no doubt it was from his fidelity to duty and his constant union with God that he drew his supernatural gifts. It might seem obvious to connect his nights of prayer with the wonders that he worked; and the circumstances of at least one of the miracles wrought by him authoritatively confirm such an assumption.

Settimia Bentorati had implored St. Felix again and again to cure her of an illness which was slowly consuming her life; but as often as she asked him, humility or some secret monition made him refuse. But one night, as she lay on her bed of suffering, Settimia's eyes were opened, and she beheld the Saint praying in the church of the Capuchins. Turning to the woman who was attending on her, she told her confidently that she would soon be cured, as she had seen Brother Felix praying for her. True enough; next day he visited her, and, without exchanging a word with her, knelt by her bedside and hung one of his little crosses round her neck. "Give glory to the Cross of Christ and that alone," said he as he left her, relieved from all suffering.

CHAPTER XIV

THE LABOURER'S HIRE

HUS did the Saint's life go on until, in what was presumed to be his seventy-fifth year, God decreed that its long monotony should be broken, and the hour of rest be struck. The time had at last come for the faithful servant to receive his wage, and for the unlettered, toil-worn lay-brother to reign in glory. The exquisite humility of His servant was manifest to the Omniscience of God, and His ways with Felix were not such as they are with most. Whereas, as a rule, God allows even His saints to remain uncertain to the last about their predestination to heaven, and purifies their souls by keeping them in a state of holy, trembling fear until the great moment when faith is lost in sight, with St. Felix He did otherwise.

As the Saint knelt one night in prayer God spoke to him in vision, and revealed to him that the hour of death was at hand, and with it that of glory. He even made known to him beforehand the veneration which would be paid to him after death, and showed him various little details which would accompany the cultus, each one of which was verified.

This revelation filled St. Felix's soul with such intense, childlike joy, that he could not keep his secret to himself. Sometimes, when he met one of his companions in the passage, he would throw his arms around him in a transport of delight, saying: "Paradise, brother, paradise. Oh pray that it may not be long!" A spirit of reverent reserve kept him from relating in detail the revelation he had received, but he could not help betraying himself, and letting that transpire which was the constant theme of his thoughts. He sometimes threw out hints of what was in store for him in a characteristic, and often playful, manner.

"Poor Giovanni," said he to the steward of Alessandro Olgiati, who had for years been one of his benefactors, "I shall not come bothering you any more and tease you to fetch me the alms which your master has never refused me. Be kind to the brother who will succeed me, and treat him as well as you have treated me. I promise you I will not be ungrateful." Giovanni was sorely puzzled by the Saint's manner of speaking. "But, brother," he expostulated, "why will you not come here any more? Have I displeased or neglected you? If you give up coming here my master will suspect that I have not treated you well; and so great is his devotion to you that he will discharge me from his service." "Have no fear, Giovanni," replied St. Felix; "though I speak nothing but the truth when I tell you that, for reasons best known to myself, I shall not come here any more. Farewell, Giovanni, and pray God to hasten the hour of His mercies." The steward understood by these words that Brother Felix had been alluding to his approaching death, and, falling on his knees before him, kissed his hand, unable to utter a word for weeping. And St. Felix, being also too moved to speak, left him without further farewell.

His great joy at the prospect of death, added to his minute foreknowledge of the honour which would be afterwards paid him, led him to say and do things which some of his friends thought whimsical. About a month before his death the Saint paid a visit to his friend Alessandro Poggi, the stone-carver, and told him that he had a favour to ask of him. "You know that you have only to speak," was Poggi's reply. "All that I have is at your disposal." "It is all very well for you to say so," pursued St. Felix, "but I assure you that this request of mine will not please you at all." "I tell you," his friend repeated, "that there is nothing in the world which I would not grant you." "Very well, then," said the Saint, pointing to a beautifully carved tomb which Alessandro had just completed, "give me that coffin." "But," stammered Poggi, in a dilemma, "that has been made to order, and I cannot give it away." "Did not I tell you that my request would not please you?" returned the Saint. "Nevertheless, I must have that coffin, and you must arrange about it somehow, as best you can."

Rather than refuse the servant of God, Poggi gave him the tomb, and St. Felix went away, his only expression of thanks being a remark that it ought to be a great pleasure to the carver to oblige his best friend. By the Saint's direction the tomb was placed in a corner of the cloister, much to the surprise of the friars, who could extract no word of explanation from their companion save that he would require it soon. There the monument was allowed to remain, for the Community regarded the old brother as a Saint, and felt sure that whatever he did, even if they could not understand it, was done by the inspiration of God.

The explanation was given after the Saint's death. Nine months after that event, when orders had been given to translate his body from the common cemetery to the chapel of St. Bonaventure, the Cardinal-protector, perceiving this carved tomb standing in the cloister, gave directions that the Saint's body should be placed in it; and all those who had been before puzzled received the explanation they had vainly asked of St. Felix.

The hints he threw out about the future were numerous. The day was approaching for the assemblage of a Chapter for the election of a new General of the Franciscans; and the Capuchin lay-brothers were discussing its probable results. "I cannot tell who will be chosen," said St. Felix when asked for his opinion. "All I do know is that I shall give my vote this time; and my voice will be so loud that all Rome will hear it." His words were remembered by his companions when, while the Chapter was being held, St. Felix's body lay exposed in the church, and every citizen—man, woman and child—was hurrying to venerate his sacred relics.

Another time, Brother Marco, an Observantine brother, met the Saint while going on his rounds, and, gazing at his sandled feet, began to tease him about a current rumour that the Pope was going to issue an order to all Franciscans to wear shoes. "The Pope can of course command what he chooses," replied St. Felix; "but nothing that he decrees will affect me. In fact I shall very

soon be making such a commotion in Rome that even the Pope
will be astounded."

Sometimes, when with very intimate friends, the Saint was
more explicit in his predictions. He was calling for alms at the
house of Giulia Cesarini, and, as he often did, began to talk to her
and her sister about death and heaven, and the necessity of being
always in a state of readiness for a summons to leave this world.
Then, unable any longer to keep his secret to himself, he went
on to say: "As for me, I am by the mercy of God approaching my
end, and every hour that I am kept waiting is like a thousand
years. When you hear of my death, rejoice, for your poor old
Brother Felix will have obtained what he desires. Farewell, my
daughters; be saints." When the two ladies heard his words they
knelt before him to kiss his hand. At first his humility prompted
him to withdraw it, but on second thoughts he accepted the
token of their veneration. "Ah, well," said he, "do as you will.
Satisfy your devotion; I will not hinder you. Here is my hand;
kiss it as you will." This was so very unlike his usual manner, that
the two sisters were left in a state of great amazement.

A day or two after this visit St. Felix fell sick of fever.
Probably he recognised in this the summons for which he had
been waiting, but, true to his invariable practice, he concealed
his illness, went about as usual begging, and increased his
austerities. However, his watchful companion, Brother Matteo,
was not to be deceived, and, seeing that the Saint was really ill,
he spoke to the infirmarian, who insisted on the old man's going
to bed. To make him more comfortable he placed a mattress on
the bed, but St. Felix positively refused to lie down till this had
been removed. Nor even then could he be prevailed on to remain
quiet, for, as soon as the infirmarian had turned his back, he got
up and crept down to the church. There he was found, unable to
move, and was carried back to the infirmary. "Ah," he protested,
"why will you not suffer me to be with my Master?"

Struggle as he might against his weakness, he knew that the
end had in reality come. "The brothers' ass has fallen down," said
he, "and so heavily this time that he will never get on his feet
again." This much he could confidentially admit, nevertheless his

warfare against the flesh had become so much a habit that even yet he could not own himself vanquished by it. "How am I?" he replied to a solicitous inquiry after his health. "Why, quite well, of course. But the ass brayed so loudly that they had to put him in straw to keep him quiet."

The little comforts—if such they can be called—which were provided for him in the infirmary caused him real pain; and the Father Guardian, seeing how the Saint's spirit of mortification caused him to frustrate every effort made to take care of him and, if possible, prolong his life, commanded him not only to remain in bed, but also to lie on the mattress provided for him. This obedience was hard, and, with mirthful self-pity, he complained of it to his companions. "How could I feel better lying like this?" he replied to the inquiries of one. "Just think, they have compelled an ass—who ought to have been thrashed till he got up—to lie down on a comfortable mattress!"

The devil was not slow to take advantage of this antipathy on the Saint's part, to try to at least disturb his peace of mind. So great indeed was the shrinking of his mortified spirit from all bodily ease that it was no difficult matter to make him think that any indulgence was a diabolical snare. "Ah," said Satan, appearing before him: "so you have given in at last!" Hearing these words, which were in consonance with his own view of the situation, the Saint got up and lay on the bare floor, where he was found by the infirmarian, who placed him back in bed. Then the devil appeared again and jeered at him for returning to his comforts, and once more the old Saint laid himself on the ground. The infirmarian having found him thus and lifted him back on his bed, rebuked him and reminded him of the obedience imposed on him by the Father Guardian.

However, the devil was not going to leave him in peace. "What!" he said, as soon as the Saint was once more left alone. "Do I find you back in bed for the third time?" "Yes," cried St. Felix, "for a third time, and, if necessary, for a tenth or a hundredth time. I lie here by obedience, and I shall die here in spite of you who suffer everlasting death on account of disobedience." Satan, being baffled, retired for a time, only to return to make one final effort to disturb the dying Saint by the suggestion that his long life of faithful service was of no avail, and that the justice of God would condemn him and banish him to everlasting punishment. "Deceiver!" cried the Saint, "who made you my judge? How dare you take on yourself that which belongs to God alone? I acknowledge but one judge, Jesus the Son of God. Depart, for you cannot touch me. All that I have done worthy of punishment, all that could cause me to be condemned, has been washed clean by the Precious Blood of my Lord Jesus Christ!"

After this St. Felix was left in peace to drink of the joy with which his heart over-brimmed. The hour for which he had longed was close at hand, and he spent the time that remained in unmixed thanksgiving. When he was informed that the end was near, and that it would be well for him to receive the last sacraments, his sole response was his favourite ejaculation, *Deo gratias.* Rousing his remaining strength, he made a fervent confession of his whole life and asked pardon of the assembled Community for what he called his many offences against them. When bidden to make ready to receive Holy Viaticum, he burst out singing the *O sacrum convivium,* and asked all present to help him to thank God.

He was then left alone with Brother Urban, and it seemed to this brother—who afterwards related faithfully all that he beheld—that faith had for St. Felix been exchanged for sight even here on earth. Seeing the Saint raise himself in bed and stretch out his arms while he uttered exclamations of wonder, Urban asked him what he saw. "I see the Mother of God," said St. Felix, "and millions of angels who fill the room with light. Shut the door, my son, lest it go." Then, recalling himself to his senses, he asked the brother to leave him alone with the saints and angels.

Urban did as he was requested, but kneeling near the door he listened to the Saint singing his favourite canticle:

> Gesù tu mi creasti
> Perché ti debbo amare.
> Io to bramo; io to chiamo
> Tanto che mi sent' il cuor mancare.

As his voice died away Urban crept back and beheld the Saint yield up his spirit, with the holy words still on his lips. This was at about five in the afternoon of Whit Monday, the 18th of May 1587.

St. Felix had left his friends, but never was loss felt more gradually, for it seemed to them that he was living in their midst for days after he had gone from them. Even in outward semblance he remained with them, or rather he was restored to them such as some might have remembered him more than half a century before. As soon as he had breathed forth his spirit a wondrous and beauteous change came over his body. The old man's flesh became as the flesh of a little child, and his scarred and rugged limbs as smooth and supple as a boy's. All those who beheld this phenomenon exclaimed by common consent that the transformation could be nothing save an indication of the Saint's virginal purity.

As soon as the news of his death passed beyond the convent, visitors began to pour in. Cardinals, princes, and other grand folk invaded the humble cell where St. Felix lay, disputing with each other for such poor objects as had been his to use. Moreover, Camilla, the Pope's sister, and other great ladies, having obtained leave to enter the enclosure, venerated his sacred remains. Outside, the populace clamoured for admission, scaled the walls, over-ran the cloister and garden, and threatened to batter down the doors which kept them from their dear Brother Felix. In order to restore order the Father Guardian had to promise that the body should be exposed in the church, where it was laid, protected by a railing and guarded by about a dozen men, whose services the friars enlisted.

However, iron grilles and stalwart sentries were but weak bulwarks against what may be called the fury of popular devotion. "Fra Felice is dead," wrote Father Bordini of the Roman Oratory to Tarugi at Naples, "and all the city laments him. They kept him three days unburied, with great concourse of people, and such devotion that they left him neither habit nor beard." Thrice had the Saint's habit to be renewed, the two first having been torn off shred by shred; and it was all the friars could do to save the body itself from desecration at the hands of devotees. It was evident to the people that their Brother Felix still lived, and lived for them, for miracles poured from his relics even as they had in life poured from his healing hand. Those who were sick in soul or body made their way to his feet and came away leaving their burden behind them; and the crowd, regardless of all warnings and prohibitions, cried out with one voice: "Blessed Felix, pray for us."

All this commotion was thoroughly distasteful to the humble Capuchins. None knew better than they that their brother was a Saint, but the turmoil and parade offended their poverty and simplicity. It was only at the end of four days that the Cardinal-protector allowed them to bury him, and even then they were not permitted to do so in their own way, for they were compelled to enclose the body in a lead coffin, in case any further proceedings should be necessary. This done, they hoped that they might at least be spared further publicity, but not so. The miracles wrought by St. Felix's intercession were so numerous, and the devotion of the people so increasing, that Cardinal Santorio decided to remove the coffin from the friars' cemetery, and place it in the chapel of St. Bonaventure. To do this some sort of tomb was necessary, and then it was that the reason of the Saint's strange action about Poggi's monument was made manifest. Seeing this standing unused in the cloister, the Cardinal directed that it should be converted into a tomb for St. Felix.

While the Saint's resting-place in the church was being made ready his coffin remained exposed, and his unfailing care for the needs of his fellow-citizens was shown in a new way. While Brother Urban, who had been with the Saint when he died, was watching and praying near the body, he saw a strange liquid trickling through the coffin, with which he filled a phial. He confided what had occurred to Sister Felice, who thus comes forward once more as a recipient of the Saint's secrets. Together, she and Urban applied the beneficent balm to the sick, and by its means wonderful cures were wrought, characterised by the same bountiful profusion which had marked his miracles in life.

But the phial was small, and the precious store soon exhausted. However, Sister Felice's sense of gratitude determined her to do her best to obtain more, and, taking Cardinal Maffei's sister into her confidence, they obtained permission to remain in St. Bonaventure's chapel when the church was closed. Then, taking an auger, they made a hole right through Poggi's beautifully carved stone and through the leaden coffin, and by means of a sponge fixed on wire obtained a supply of the wonder-working balm, with which cures were effected as before.

The miracles were known to all, but the instrument of them was kept secret by the two ladies and Brother Urban. But the affair coming to the ears of Sixtus V, he ordered an inquiry to be made, and the three friends thought it better to confess to their deed, with the result that the Saint's coffin was opened, and a strict medical examination made and recorded.

When it was made known that the servant of God's body still remained uncorrupt, and when renewed miracles followed the examination, all Rome clamoured for his canonisation. But the Capuchins were backward and poor, and took no steps to promote the cause. Thus it was not till October, 1625, that Felix was beatified by Urban VIII; nor till nearly a century later, on May 28, 1712, that Clement XI caused him to be numbered among the Saints, and pronounced his canonisation.

9 781953 746252